Inspiring stories and practical insights for

Worshiping God in the Hard Times

by Tom Kraeuter

"But understand this, that in the last days
there will come times of difficulty."
(2 Timothy 3:1)

Worshiping God in the Hard Times
© 2009 Training Resources, Inc.
    65 Shepherd's Way
    Hillsboro, MO 63050
    (636) 7894522
    www.training-resources.org

Co-published by Training Resources and
    Bent Whisker Press
    Shoreline WA
    (206) 914-3556
    publisher@bentwhiskerpress.com

ISBN for you: 978-0-9842666-0-9

Dedication:

I humbly dedicate this book to my dear friends,
Daryl Roth and Jerry Waggoner.
Thanks so much for choosing to walk with me
through the difficult situations of life.
You guys have meant so much to me in more ways
than you know. Thank you.

Thanks to:

My friends, Laurie Mellinger and John Barcanic,
for reviewing the manuscript and offering amazing
insights that really helped strengthen the final product.

Jennifer Brody for great editing
and again challenging my thinking.
I absolutely love what you do with my writing!

Connie Wood for proofing the initial draft.
Thanks for your diligence.

Fran Moore for the final proofing. Great job!

To the close friends and the many others I have met
who have shared tremendously inspiring stories of
worshiping God during difficult times. Thank you so
much for opening yourselves to me and allowing me a
glimpse of what God did on the inside.

*And special thanks to my wonderful family, especially
my wife Barbara, for again allowing me the time and
space to complete this manuscript. You are the best!*

Other Books by Tom Kraeuter

Reflecting God's Mercy in an Unmerciful World

Becoming a True Worshiper

The Missing Element of Worship

Oh Grow Up!
The Everyday Miracle of Becoming More Like Jesus

Worship Is... What?!
Rethinking Our Ideas About Worship

If Standing Together Is So Great, Why Do We Keep Falling Apart?

Living Beyond the Ordinary
Developing an Extraordinary Relationship with God

Guiding Your Church Through a Worship Transition

Times of Refreshing: A Worship Ministry Devotional

Keys to Becoming an Effective Worship Leader

Developing an Effective Worship Ministry

The Worship Leader's Handbook

Things They Didn't Teach Me in Worship Leading School

CONTENTS

Section 1 – What it looks like to worship God in the hard times

Section 2 – How to worship God during the hard times

Section 1

What It Looks Like to Worship God in the Hard Times

A Proper Perspective

I recently conducted a retreat for those who lead congregational worship in churches across North America. It was two full days of worship and prayer, fellowship and teaching. Most of the folks who attended, although tired, were still on a mountain-top from the recently completed Easter season. Some, however, were struggling. Budget cuts. Lay-offs. Criticism from leaders as well as from congregation members. One man had just been released from his position because a few who had opposed his initial hiring had wormed their ways into positions of authority in the congregation. Another, whose adult son had recently walked away from his faith, was devastated. How could he stand before his congregation when his own son had abandoned all that he had tried to instill into him? There were others—too many stories to share—who were broken in spirit and feeling crushed by recent situations and circumstances. A few of these leaders looked as though they needed to be carried in on a stretchers.

Something happened, though, during our time together. By the end of those two days, things had changed dramatically. Don't misunderstand. The people were still returning to their same situations, but their outlooks had been altered. Hour upon hour of gazing on the beauty of the Lord—of worshiping Him—had amazingly changed their points of view. The situations were still just as real, but now they were in the proper perspective. They realized that God indeed was still in control. Their situations didn't catch Him by surprise. Those who had been beaten down now realized anew that the Lord was bigger than their situations and circumstances.

Worship can do that in our lives. When we fix our eyes on God, things change. Not necessarily the scenario itself, but our perspective is altered in dramatic ways.

My family and I live in the St. Louis, Missouri, area. Because of the close proximity, we have many times visited the Gateway Memorial Arch. It's a massive structure made of stainless steel and concrete. A few times while visiting there I've seen people taking pictures that were different from the usual shots of the Arch. The first time I saw someone taking one of these photos, it took a moment for me to figure out what was happening. Someone stands on the hill just up from the base of the Arch, hands in the air as though holding something up, while someone else shoots the photo. The final effect is that it appears that the person is holding up the Arch. In fact, if the lighting is right and the photographer has done a good job, the final picture can make it look very realistic. The person appears to be nearly as big as the structure itself. That's quite a feat, since the Arch is more than 600 feet tall!

You know, just like in those photos, our perspective can alter how reality appears. No one could possibly be 600 feet tall, and the Gateway Memorial Arch is certainly not just over six feet tall, but the photo sure makes it look that way. We know that it would be impossible for a single human being to hold up a massive structure of steel and concrete. However, reality becomes skewed by the odd perspective.

When you or I are facing tough times in life—whether a job loss, death of a loved one, a debilitating disease, ongoing problems with family or other relationships, or any of a myriad of other possibilities, big and small—those events can seem way out of proportion. As we stare intently at those situations, they can appear massive. They look so big and so grave that we feel overwhelmed by them, crushed by their weight. In the midst of such scenarios nothing else is even visible. That situation is so gigantic that it fills the frame of our mind from one side to other. There is often no room left for anything more. From our perspective, nothing else seems anywhere near as significant as the catastrophe staring us in the face.

If you will allow me a moment to be extremely candid, that entire last paragraph is a skewed perspective on reality. It's like those photos of the Arch. I'm not suggesting that the situation is not real. It may be very real, and it may indeed seem overwhelming. But just like the person in the photo seems nearly 600 feet tall, it's really not as it appears, because the perspective is all wrong.

I have faced trying times when I just wanted to hide away. I was overwhelmed. On the surface it appeared as though the situation would consume me because of the sheer size of it. Yet, in those moments when I've taken the time to put my gaze upon God—to worship Him even though I didn't necessarily feel like it—the change was monumental. Don't misunderstand. The problem didn't go away. In fact, there have been times when the problem actually got worse. But my perspective changed. I began to see how big God is and how little—in comparison—the problem is. As I did what Scripture commands, magnify the Lord, the situation no longer seemed nearly 600 feet tall. In fact, in comparison to God, that tragic scenario suddenly appeared tiny. It may still have hurt. I might have continued to feel the pain of heartache or loss, but it was no longer giant-sized. By choosing to fill the frame of my life with God rather than with the problem, I had regained a proper perspective. I worshiped Him, and that altered everything.

As I was reading in the book of *Psalms* recently,

I noticed a section that fascinated me. Although I had read these verses many times, I never before noticed an odd quirk. In twelve consecutive verses, three of those twelve are worded exactly the same way. Psalm 42:5, 42:11 and 43:5 all say the same thing. "Why are you cast down, O my soul, and why are you in turmoil within me? Hope in God; for I shall again praise him..."

Just a couple verses earlier the psalmist declares that his tears have been his food day and night as mockers look on and ask, "Where is your God?" Between the first and second identical verses he asks God, "Why have you forsaken me?" Later he inquires of the Lord, "Why have you rejected me?"

The psalmist's world was in chaos. He couldn't see the hand of God at work in his life. In fact, it seemed as though the Lord had abandoned him. He could not understand why God seemed silent and uncaring. The jeers of his enemies asking, "Where is your God?" must have resounded in his ears. He apparently struggled, wondering the same thing.

Yet even in the midst of this scenario he kept bringing himself back to the truth: in God there is still hope. In God there is always hope. I *will* hope in the Lord my God. Indeed, I *shall* praise Him again.

Although there was turmoil within, he recognized that he could still lift his voice in praise to the Lord. In spite of not seeing the Lord's hand at work in his situation, the psalmist chose to hope in God and praise Him anyway.

I am part of a fellowship of worship leaders who

meet regularly in the St. Louis area. Not long ago someone who is not a worship leader happened to stop in to
one of our gatherings. She told us that she wanted to
thank us. "We 'everyday folks' come in on Sunday
mornings," she said, "and you lift us before the throne
of God. Suddenly the struggles of the week disappear, at
least for a time, because you help transport us to God
through worship. Thank you."

We were stunned. Her words were a big encour-
agement. More, though, they confirm what frequently
happens as we worship the Lord. Like the old song says,
"The things of earth will grow strangely dim in the light
of His glory and grace."

Choosing to worship the Lord in the midst of
difficult times can potentially impact us in several ways.

1. Focusing on God through worship
helps us to remember how big God is
and—relatively speaking—how small
our problem is. This helps increase our
faith and confidence in the Lord.

2. Worshiping the Lord during hard times
can bring us comfort. Remembering His
mercies and compassion—and focusing
on those things—offer more consolation
than we can generally imagine. And since
true worship involves the totality of our
being (mind, body, will, emotions) it can
potentially help bring restoration to all of
those areas.

3. For me, one of the major results of choosing to worship God when life is difficult is that it gets my focus off of me and onto the Lord. I am reminded once again that life is not all about me. Everything, ultimately, is all about God.
4. Finally, making the choice to worship the Lord while I am hurting reminds me that God will use even this hard time to bring about good for me. In the final result, everything I am facing will be leveraged into the wonderful, glorious reward He has waiting for me in eternity.

Author and worship leader Phil Christensen is a gifted wordsmith. He wrote a song, *More Than Enough*, that says it well. The lyrics begin, "More than this tiny trial, more than this minor mountain, more than this giant that I see…" Are you facing any "tiny" trials? "Minor" mountains? Giants? If so, lift your heart and your voice and worship the One who has promised never to leave us or forsake us. The One who, when this life is over, will take us home with Him…forever. It may not change the situation, but it may well change your heart. And that will change everything.

One final thought before we dive in. Prior to publication of this book, I asked some people to review the manuscript. One of those people really helped me to understand something that hadn't been very clear in the initial writing. There is a big difference between situations that are merely inconveniences and those that are real tragedies. If I inadvertently forget my cell phone at home when I run to the store, that's an inconvenience. If my son dies in a car accident, that's a tragedy.

The truth, though, is that knowing exactly where to draw the line between those two extremes can get tricky. People are different. Not everyone will respond the same way to the same situation. An event that might send one person into a tail spin may not be a big deal for someone else. Part of this is because of our backgrounds. It seems safe to say that someone who survived a Nazi concentration camp would find the majority of non-life-threatening issues trivial. A person who has had a life filled with tragic experiences is less likely to be ruffled by things that someone else deems extremely difficult. On the other hand, a teenager who has never encountered any serious trials might find misplacing his cell phone a major tragedy. It all has to do with background, experience and personality.

The bottom line is this: Some of the stories in this book are situations of epic proportions, regardless of your background and experience. Others might possibly seem trivial to you. Regardless of the situation, though, we should still worship the Lord in the midst of whatever difficulty we might be facing—large or small.

Throughout the pages of this book, I hope to engulf us in stories and Scripture passages that will alter our thinking and our actions. Like so many who have walked before us, we need to learn to worship God during the hard times.

In the first section of this book, I will endeavor to paint a picture of what it looks like to worship God in the hard times. In the second section, I will offer what the professor who taught us preaching and teaching in seminary called "the practical how-to's." In other words, we will look at how we can make worship in the hard times a reality. I pray that God uses these words to draw our hearts—yours and mine—more and more to Himself even in the midst of difficulties. ❖

Worship in the Midst of Tragedy

I first met Bonnie Henady at a worship seminar I was presenting in Oklahoma. After the seminar, she introduced herself and told me that what I had shared had really helped her cope with a situation in her life. She then proceeded to tell me a story about her son.

Sixteen-year-old Jonathan Henady had a zeal for life. He was popular with his classmates at school, but that was not surprising. Jonathan never met a stranger. He had an engaging way about him that caused everyone, young and old alike, to like him.

One Saturday, Jonathan and his entire family spent the evening at a special fundraising event at their church. A strong Christian family from a rural area, Roger and Bonnie and their four children, Jonathan, Stephen, Hannah and Joshua, spent a great deal of time together at church events. That night, after everything was cleaned up, Jonathan asked his folks if he could go see his girlfriend. He promised to be home by 9:00 PM. His parents agreed. For nearly his whole life—and even more so in the past year—Jonathan had proven to be a very trustworthy young man. They had absolutely no reservations about allowing him to go.

When Jonathan had not arrived home by 9:15, his parents called his cell phone. It immediately clicked to voice mail. The same thing happened at 9:30. Jonathan was very conscientious, and it was extremely unusual for him not to let someone know when he was going to be late. His mother was worried.

It was nearly 10:30 when their cell phone rang. It was Roger's mother, Jonathan's grandmother. The local hospital had called her because they could not get through to the Henady's home phone. Jonathan had been in an automobile accident. They needed to go to the hospital.

As the news sunk in, Roger prayed, "Jesus, he is in Your arms. Take care of him."

Roger and Bonnie quickly got the other children together and left for the hospital. Although it was not a long drive, to Bonnie it seemed like eternity.

Roger's parents and the hospital chaplain met the Henadys when they arrived. As yet, no one had any information about the extent of Jonathan's injuries. All they could do was wait. Others came to the hospital: the youth minister from their church, some of Jonathan's friends, family. It wasn't long, though, before the doctor walked into the waiting room.

"Mr. and Mrs. Henady, your son has some internal injuries. His liver is damaged. One of his lungs is collapsed. There don't seem to be any broken bones. That's good. But we need to operate right away. It will probably take at least two hours."

Bonnie was in shock. Visions of Jonathan serving and helping at the fundraiser just hours before raced through her mind. Now the doctor was talking about surgery. *What had he said about internal injuries?* She just nodded her head in agreement.

After the doctor left, the hospital security guard approached the Henadys and handed them the things Jonathan had in his possession when he entered the hospital—wallet, keys, girlfriend's class ring—pretty much everything except his clothes. Bonnie and Roger stared at the items. *Was this really happening?*

It was just 45 minutes later when the doctor, visibly shaken, returned to the waiting room. "Mr. and Mrs. Henady, I'm sorry," he said. "Jonathan was a very muscular boy, and because of that we really couldn't tell the extent of the injuries. When we opened him up, the damage done to the arteries and the internal bleeding were just too much. We lost him. We did everything we could. I'm so very sorry."

The silence was palpable. No one moved. No one spoke. Then, just as quickly, the quiet was shattered by the crying of ten-year-old Hannah. Her tears came in great torrents. Her brother was gone.

Bonnie, on the other hand, was too numb to cry. Maybe numb is too kind a word. Hadn't she just hugged Jonathan a few hours ago? How could he be—it wasn't really possible, was it—*dead*? Shock staved off any tears.

The anesthesiologist slowly approached the family and asked if they wanted to see Jonathan. Grief stricken, Roger and his parents went first. The youth minister had taken Stephen out in the hallway, so Bonnie and Hannah were left alone in the waiting room. Bonnie held Hannah in her arms, and, finally, she cried. "We lost him, Hannah. We lost him!"

As Bonnie related the story to me, I was overwhelmed with emotion. I could picture Bonnie hugging her young daughter to herself and crying. Even worse, my youngest son was about Jonathan's age at the time. Honestly, Jonathan sounded just like him. Fun, outgoing, the life of the party, very muscular—the description fit my Stephen perfectly. I wondered how I would have reacted in such a situation. Although I was completely caught up in the emotion of the story—I felt the pain, sensed the grief—nothing prepared me for what she said next.

As they sat alone in the hospital waiting room, Bonnie and Hannah stopped crying. However, they didn't replace their crying with screams of pain or with empty blank stares. Instead, they began to softly sing of the Lord's love. In the midst of their grief, they vocalized their confidence in the God Who loved them passionately.

I was dumbfounded. Again I wondered, *How would I have reacted? Would I have worshiped in the midst of such tragedy?* I didn't know for sure.

Truth be told, none of us knows with certainty the answer to such a question until we have the opportunity to find out for sure in real life. Of course, I'd like to think I would lift my voice in a confident affirmation of God's love even when my heart is breaking. But would I? I just don't know.

King David

I really like the stories of King David in the Old Testament. In many ways his life is a great example for us to emulate. Yet, there are a few instances from David's life that serve better as bad examples for us. Among those, David's relationship with Bathsheba would have to be the worst.

One day, after his army had gone off to battle, David happened to catch a glimpse of Bathsheba bathing. That was all it took. As he stood gazing at her nakedness, David decided he wanted to have her. He desired her. Unfortunately, lust and sovereign authority are a very powerful combination. David got what he wanted. In the end, though, he ended up with more than he bargained for. Bathsheba wound up pregnant from their encounter. Even that, though, might not have been such a big problem except for the little matter of Uriah, her husband. But that was only a minor obstacle for a king. David would simply make him go away. You know, have him "taken care of." Of course, David was creative. He would make it look like an accident. It certainly wouldn't be blatant. No firing squad, nor even a hired assassin. No, Uriah was inadvertently—and conveniently—killed in the midst of battle.

It was actually a pretty effective plan. It worked. Well, almost. David overlooked one small piece of the puzzle. Somehow, David seemed to have temporarily forgotten about God. He neglected to realize that the Lord had seen the entire incident. From the initial lust-filled glance to the intentional murder of Uriah, God knew the whole scenario. Although David did a good job of covering his tracks, the One who knows all and sees all was on to him. The Most High saw the tricks and shenanigans, the lust and deception, the plotting and murder, and He was determined to confront David with what he had done.

The Lord sent a messenger to David to let him know that his actions had not gone unnoticed. Although David endeavored to at least somewhat redeem the situation by marrying Bathsheba, God was still very displeased with him. So the Lord sent Nathan the prophet to tell David so. To David's credit, he received the prophet's rebuke and repented of what he had done. And—this should go without saying but let's say it anyway, just to be clear—the Lord forgave David.

As a result, David and God were back on good terms when the baby was born. Nevertheless, the baby became gravely ill, so sick that death seemed inevitable.

Then David, as any good father would have, cried out to the Lord on behalf of his sick child. Though David was far from perfect (Did I mention his very serious lust problem?), he was still a compassionate guy. If you read the story (2 Samuel 11-12), it is obvious that David loved this child. For several days he prayed and fasted, asking God to heal the little one. In the end, though, the baby succumbed to that final foe, death. What a heart-rending experience that must have been.

I missed the birth of our daughter, Amy. I had been there for each of the two boys, right in the birthing room, helping my wife to focus and stay calm. Those were amazing experiences. We had the same idea for number three, but it didn't quite work according to our plan. (Amy is now a teenager and has always, seemingly, had her own timetable.) So she arrived two weeks early when I was out of town. I was flying back home that evening and would be on hand for the next twenty-five days. But Amy decided to surprise us and make her appearance sooner than expected. As a result, I arrived at the hospital several hours after she was born.

The initial rush of seeing her and holding her for the first time are still vivid memories in my mind. Her bright eyes. Her tiny hands. That little girl captured this daddy's heart immediately. I loved her the moment I laid eyes on her. She was a precious gift from God. I cannot even begin to fathom what it would have been like for me if Amy had died a week later. What an unthinkably devastating experience that would have been.

That's exactly what happened to David's child, though. In fact, his experience may well have been quite similar to mine. Customs of the day would have left David out of the actual birthing process. Most likely, he would not have seen the child until sometime after the birth. Would David have been immediately smitten by this infant, as I was with Amy? Of course, we don't know for sure. However, nearly any parent will testify that it is certainly likely.

I have met people whose babies died. Sometimes their lives are turned inside out. They may be mad at God. They could be mad at themselves. Whatever the root cause, something is wrong in their lives from the moment it happens and for a long time to come. I have encountered people who were traumatized for years as a result of the death of an infant child.

That's why I find David's reaction even more amazing. "Then David arose from the earth and washed and anointed himself and changed his clothes. *And he went into the house of the LORD and worshiped*" (2 Samuel 12:20, author's emphasis).

To see the baby that I loved so dearly and so deeply… lying dead. Would my first reaction be to worship God? That sweet infant—the product of an intimate union between my wife and me—now lifeless and cold, the skin a pale bluish color. Could I, after gazing on such a sight, then turn to my Creator and lift my voice in songs of worship? David did.

Please recognize that Scripture does not say that David danced exuberantly in this instance. He probably did not jump around, shouting with gladness. More likely his worship took on a somewhat contemplative tone. He was, after all, in mourning. David was experiencing true heartfelt pain. It likely gripped him to the core. This ordeal was not a fun-filled experience for David. But make no mistake: In the midst of his grief, David still worshiped.

Eugene Petersen, in his introduction to the book of *Job* in *The Message*, said this, "Perhaps the greatest mystery in suffering is how it can bring a person into the presence of God in a state of worship, full of wonder, love and praise. Suffering does not inevitably do that, but it does it far more often than we would expect."

Of course, difficult times don't *always* drive people to God. Sometimes such events drive people in the opposite direction. Actually, it seems to me that whenever we encounter a tragic situation, we have a choice. We can allow the event to push us *away* from the Lord, or we can let it propel us *toward* Him. We get to choose whether the incident causes us to run away from or run to the Lord. And—make no mistake—the choice truly is ours.

In the midst of difficulty, will you choose to allow your heart to follow hard after God? Or will you choose to close your heart off to Him? Only you can make the choice. ❖

Worship in Prison

After his conversion, the Apostle Paul traveled extensively telling everyone who would listen about the good news of the Lord Jesus Christ. During his second major evangelistic journey, Paul, accompanied by Silas, was in Philippi. While they were on their way to a prayer meeting in Philippi, a demon-possessed slave girl accosted them. She apparently followed them around for several days and kept shouting, "These men are servants of the Most High God, who proclaim to you the way of salvation" (Acts 16:17).

For such a thing to happen once might be novel. A couple of times might be bearable. But for her to repeatedly shout day after day, I would think that it might have a tendency to get monotonous. It could easily become annoying and even wearying. If I were in Paul's shoes, I would assuredly want the noise to cease. Apparently, Paul felt the same way. He was finally exasperated enough that he turned to the woman and said, "I command you in the name of Jesus Christ to come out of her" (Acts 16:18).

And just that simply, the demon came out.

The owners of the slave girl, however, were not happy with this turn of events. That demonic spirit's predilection for fortune-telling had been a major source of income for them. Now that the demon was gone, so was their source of income. So they grabbed Paul and Silas and dragged them off to the city officials. These slave owners were not about to let this offense go unpunished. Interestingly, though, when the charges were brought, there was no mention of the slave girl nor the now-absent demonic spirit. Instead, the girl's owners said, "These men are Jews, and they are disturbing our city. They advocate customs that are not lawful for us as Romans to accept or practice" (Acts 16:20-21).

It seems likely to me that if these folks had told the actual story—including the missing demon—they probably would have been laughed at. Can't you picture the scene? "Umm, let me get this straight. They cast a demon out of your slave girl and now you want them punished?" Perhaps they realized this. So instead of mentioning the actual specific facts, they dramatized the event with generalities.

You see, they weren't looking for an actual court

hearing. No, they wanted to be sure that Paul and Silas got what they deserved. So rather than quietly stating their case to the city officials, they loudly proclaimed an accusation that was sure to stir up the mob. They wanted to cause a riot. They definitely got what they wanted.

Scripture tells us that the crowd joined in on the attack. We don't know for certain how many people were there, but the Greek word literally means "multitude." Suffice it to say that there were a whole bunch of folks there attacking Paul and Silas. That doesn't sound like much fun to me.

Then the city officials tore Paul's and Silas' clothes off of them and gave orders that they be beaten with rods. With the mob mentality already in full swing, those blows were not just light taps. There can be no doubt that the guys with the rods were endeavoring to cause serious pain. In fact, the text tells us that they "inflicted many blows upon them." Then it goes on to say that they "threw" Paul and Silas into prison. The Greek word literally means to "throw," as in toss through the air, most likely with a thud on the ground at the end. And when they landed with that thud on the ground, the jailer put them into the inner cell and fastened their feet in stocks.

Try to imagine this scenario in your mind. Paul and Silas, beaten and bloody.[1] Probably naked. Tossed through the air. Dragged into the inner prison—commentaries suggest maximum security—and feet fastened in stocks. What a horrendous predicament! All because they cast out a demon. How would you react in such a situation? I honestly can't say for sure how I would react, but I can imagine some less-than-positive scenarios.

However, the Bible does record how Paul and Silas responded. It's such an outlandish response, though, that most people would never believe it. Of course, I realize that you are probably familiar with this story so you already know what happened. But, pretend for a moment that you don't know this story. All you know is what I've shared so far. What do you honestly think would be the normal reaction of Paul and Silas— or you and me—to such treatment?

Whining? *It's not fair!*

Screaming? *HELP!!!*

Complaining to God? *Lord, we were doing Your work. How could You let this happen?!*

Wouldn't these be likely scenarios? Of course they would. We can well imagine any or all of these responses.

But you and I both know that's not what happened.

"About midnight Paul and Silas were praying and singing hymns to God" (Acts 16:25). The Greek word translated as "hymn" actually implies celebration or praise. They were praising the Lord! After being beaten and brutalized, they sang. Bleeding and in pain, they chose to give thanks to God. Doesn't that seem just a bit outlandish?

Or maybe—just maybe—it was the *best* option for Paul and Silas. Perhaps, too, it is the right choice for you and me. ❖

Musical Instruments
Hanging on the Trees

There can be no doubt that we, indeed, get to choose how we respond during difficult times. Will we turn toward God or away from Him? Will we worship or whine? One of the stories from Israel's history illustrates this point well.

In Old Testament times, when one nation conquered another, many of the defeated people generally were paraded off to the homeland of their captors. Their new position, of course, was to serve. A few of the captives—the brightest and the best—were sometimes put into advisory positions. Most, though, became slaves. As would be expected, some masters—just as some people in general—were more benevolent than others. However, slaves who previously had been an enemy usually were not the recipients of kind treatment. Normally they were given the least pleasant jobs. The things that nobody else wanted to do became their lot. Beyond this, constant and ongoing ridicule, because of their defeat, was quite common. With very few exceptions, their former rank in society did not offer them much in the way of help or relief. Even the formerly wealthy were now expected to clean the latrines and dig the ditches. The most ignoble of occupations were thrust upon them, and the most insulting mockings became their constant companions. Lives often were turned completely upside down overnight.

The Babylonian captivity was just such a scenario for the Israelites.[1] The invading horde came in and won a swift and decisive victory. The Israelites were defeated and carried as captives off to Babylon. What must life have been like for those unfortunate Israelites?

Imagine for a moment that you were among those captured. Maybe you were a carpenter or a potter. You might have been a nursing mother. You could have been a wealthy businessman or a poor farmer. Whatever your former position, your entire life would have been radically and uncompromisingly altered. Maybe after your first day of hard labor—especially if you were unaccustomed to hard labor—your muscles would ache like you had never experienced before; yet calling in sick the next day was not an option. You would be forced to do it all over again, repeatedly, like it or not.

Any slowing of your pace due to your aching muscles surely would have been seen as insubordination. Would that have been cause for a beating? If so, would they use canes or a whip or some other torturous device? We don't know all these details for certain, but it's safe to say that life as you once knew it was over. Completely and irrevocably over.

In the midst of this scenario, how would you react? Would you wonder if God had abandoned you? If so, would you wonder why? Would you be mad at Him? Would you be certain He must be mad at you? And could you, in the middle of such distress and hardship, still worship Him?

These are the same questions that the Israelites needed to grapple with, as expressed in Psalm 137. They had been captured by the Babylonians and carried off to that foreign land. There, in the midst of their captivity, they began to lament:

> By the waters of Babylon, there we sat down and wept, when we remembered Zion. On the willows there we hung up our lyres. For there our captors required of us songs, and our tormentors, mirth, saying, "Sing us one of the songs of Zion!" (Psalm 137:1-3).

The Israelites were devastated. Their new positions in life caused them to weep. They didn't like it. They were so distraught they even hung up their lyres, their instruments of worship. Then, as though they weren't feeling badly enough already, their captors began to ridicule them. "Come on... sing us one of those songs that we've heard so much about. You know, those songs about your, ummm... 'god'." *Snicker, snicker.*

Nothing like rubbing a little salt in the wound, eh?

Here is an interesting side note. When slaves were captured, they were usually not allowed to bring along any personal possessions. If possessions were allowed, they would generally have been only things the captors thought to be of primary usefulness. Clothing. Tools for working. Perhaps cooking utensils. Certainly a conquering army would not have considered something as subjective as a musical instrument to be worthwhile. It seems to me, then, that the only way they would have been able to bring along those lyres was to beg their captors to allow it. It would seem that the Israelites really wanted those instruments.

So when the Babylonians demanded that the Israelites use those instruments, how did they respond? What did they say to their captors? Here it is, pretty much the way they said it, but you should most likely try to read it with a bit of whine. "How shall we sing the LORD's song in a foreign land?" (Psalm 137:4).[2] Can't you hear their lament? Don't you sense the whiny tone they surely must have used while saying this? They certainly wouldn't have asked the question with a cocky confidence. They were distraught, perhaps confused.

The truth is, though, that they made the wrong choice. Don't misunderstand. Refusing to sing was the easy choice. It may have even been, on the surface, the logical choice. After all, it made sense in light of their circumstances. Still, it was the wrong choice.

So, what, you might ask, would the right choice have been? Simple. They should have snatched their lyres off those willow trees and lifted their voices in a song of praise to their God. They should have done exactly as their captors requested. Oh, it may not have changed their outward circumstances. They most likely still would have been slaves. However, it may well have changed their hearts. And that, my friend, could have changed everything.

It is possible that the Israelites did sing at this point. As slaves, they could have been forced to do their masters' bidding. Refusal may have meant dire consequences. However, it is clear from the text that even if they did sing, they didn't do it willingly. No this was a song without heart. It was words and music with no conviction about the truth they were singing.

Please recognize that I'm not suggesting that willingly and wholeheartedly singing praise to God would necessarily have been an easy thing to do. In fact, it may well have been far more difficult than even the harsh slave-tasks they were performing. When lives are turned upside down, abruptly devastated by situations and circumstances, worship may not be the immediate natural response, but it is still the appropriate response.

In his excellent book about the life of David in the Old Testament, noted author Chuck Swindoll phrased it like this:

Never mind how beautiful or how pitiful
you sound. Sing loud enough to drown
out those defeating thoughts that normally clamor for attention. Release yourself
from that cage of introspective reluc-
tance. SING OUT! SING OUT! You're
not auditioning for the church choir;
you're making melody with your heart to
the Lord your God![3]

When your life seems to be crumbling, put your
eyes on your Creator and Redeemer and choose to trust
Him. Even though the situation seems not to warrant
such trust, make the choice to worship Him. Glorifying
God is always the appropriate decision.

Before the Captivity

Just prior to the Babylonian invasion, the Lord
raised up a prophet in Israel named Habakkuk. This
prophet had witnessed his nation becoming severely
corrupt and was distressed by all that he saw. In the first
chapter of the book that bears his name, Habakkuk
describes the scene for us. Violence, strife and con-
tention were apparently commonplace. Those in authority were dishonest, perverting justice. As a result, the
law was paralyzed, and the wicked trampled on the
rights of the righteous. It was not a pretty picture.

This section of Scripture is short on specifics, so
let's try to use our imaginations to fill in some of the
blanks. When I read the first section of the book of

Habakkuk, it reminds me of Gotham City in the movie, *Batman Returns*. The government was so corrupt that no one even understood the true meaning of justice. Criminals were set free and upstanding citizens harassed. The streets were unsafe day or night. If you have never seen *Batman Returns*, you might have another scene playing through your mind. Lots of movies depict full-blown, wholesale corruption and evil. Choose your most vivid recollection. That's the picture being described in the first section of Habakkuk.

In the midst of this perversity, Habakkuk cries out to the Lord. In essence he asks, "How long, O Lord, will You allow this to go on? Won't You bring this wickedness to an end soon?" The prophet was frustrated. He was apparently a righteous man, and he knew that God was righteous. He couldn't understand how God could permit such licentiousness to continue.

Whatever response Habakkuk might have thought possible from the Lord, he surely could not have expected the response he received. If the prophet had taken quill and parchment in hand and listed all possible scenarios, the actual answer that God gave would not have made it into the top one-hundred answers. In his wildest imaginations—or even his worst nightmares—Habakkuk could not have contemplated such a response. The Lord informed the prophet that He was indeed about to put an end to Israel's perversions. To accomplish this, He was sending the Babylonians to conquer Israel.

What?! Habakkuk must have been stunned.

After all, the Israelites were bad, but the Babylonians were worse. Israel was evil, but Babylon was evil to the nth degree. Surely he must have misunderstood what the Lord was saying. Not Babylon. Anyone but Babylon.

Indeed Habakkuk had not misunderstood. That evil empire would be the means by which God would endeavor to turn the hearts of His people back to Himself.

The prophet knew, though, what this would mean for Israel in the physical realm. He had heard the stories of other lands where the Babylonians had invaded. They not only took many captives for slaves, but they also devastated the land. What they could take—food and livestock—they took. What they could not take—fields, orchards, homes—they destroyed. By the time the invading horde left, those who remained would find it nearly impossible to eke out a living.

Habakkuk understood the destruction that was to come. The scene that he had described there in Israel suddenly didn't seem nearly as bleak as the prophet had thought. The scene that loomed on the horizon—the invading Babylonian army—must have appeared a thousand times worse.

Yet, it is against this backdrop—this unthinkable scenario—that the prophet made one of the most resounding declarations of worship found anywhere in Scripture:

> Though the fig tree should not blossom,
> nor fruit be on the vines, the produce of

the olive fail and the fields yield no food,
the flock be cut off from the fold and there
be no herd in the stalls, yet I will rejoice
in the LORD; I will take joy in the God of
my salvation (Habakkuk 3:17-18).

Regardless of what happens—irrespective of what it looks like on the surface—I will still choose to rejoice in my God. Babylonians or no Babylonians, food or no food, in good times or bad, I still make the choice to worship the Lord. Habakkuk refused to give in to despair, even though it may have been easy to do so. Instead, he confidently lifted his voice and worshiped the Lord, his God.

We know from history that eventually the fateful day arrived, and the Israelites were carried off into captivity. At that point, why—oh, why?!—didn't the Israelites take Habakkuk's attitude with them into their captivity? Rather than despairing, why didn't they worship? If they had, would not their labors have seemed less harsh? Would they not have found true freedom even in the midst of their physical captivity?

But they didn't. No, they left their stringed instruments hanging on the trees. They wept instead of singing. They lamented their situation instead of worshiping. What a shame. ❖

Our Worship During the
Hard Times Will Affect Others

Here's another aspect of that story about the Israelites. What effect did their refusal to worship God have on their captors? Asked another way, what impact would it have made if they had chosen to worship the Lord?

Can you imagine the stunned looks on the faces of the Babylonians? After all, the Israelites were slaves. They weren't supposed to be joyful. Why would they sing? And not just sing. Why would they lift their voices and extol the virtues of the One Who had apparently abandoned them? Such a scenario would seem ludicrous to people who don't know God. Yet, such a scenario also would have to be attractive (in the very best sense of the word) to those people.

You see, our worship can—and should—influence people around us. Whether the people around us are unbelievers or they are brothers and sisters in Christ, it makes no difference. Lifting our voices in joyful songs of praise while we are in the midst of difficult times will deeply affect others.

If *we* have confidence in the Lord at a time when *they* most need confidence, it can help change their perspective. I love the words of David in Psalm 34:

> I will extol the LORD at all times; his praise will always be on my lips. My soul will boast in the LORD; let the afflicted hear and rejoice. Glorify the LORD with me; let us exalt his name together. (Psalm 34:1-3)

In essence, David is saying, "I'm going to worship the Lord, and may those who aren't doing well—those who have been afflicted—hear my words of praise and find strength in them. Then they can worship right along with me. Come on, you guys, let's exalt the Lord, our God, together!"

My high school art teacher, Al Markworth, was very instrumental in my early spiritual formation. If not for him, I might not even be in ministry today. At the very least, I'm sure my life would have been radically different if not for his influence.

I remember once, when I was still in high school, Al burned his hand quite badly. I never saw the burns—his entire hand was bandaged—but he described it in vivid detail as only an artist could. After the description, I was glad I couldn't see it.

Have you ever had a serious burn? Not just a little red mark, but a serious flesh-searing, skin-consuming burn? It is not only painful when it happens, but for several days afterward, also. Each time the bandage is changed, it can cause a ripping and more agony. It's not at all an enjoyable process.

Although Al was in obvious pain, I still remember him *thanking God* that it happened. He said that his hand hurting helped him to remember that he was not going to have to endure eternal fire, just a minor inconvenience here. He was—as Psalm 34 says— boasting in the Lord, even while in the midst of pain.

My young mind thought, *A minor inconvenience?! I would certainly not want to endure such an inconvenience.*

It was a powerful lesson for me, one that I still remember more than thirty years later. It caused me to wonder how I would react in such a scenario. Al's willingness to glorify the Lord during a very trying time caused my heart to soften.

I remember going through a very difficult time some years ago. When I went to church that Sunday, I wasn't sure I really wanted to worship God. I don't know about you, but sometimes difficulties can cause me to wallow in self-pity. Honestly, that seems to be my default mode during trying circumstances. It certainly feels more natural to me than any other reaction. So worship was not exactly at the forefront of my thoughts as I entered the church building that Sunday morning. However, as I listened to those around me singing and pouring out their hearts to God, it affected me.

John, recently diagnosed with cancer lifted his hands to worship the Lord. Another friend, struggling through a rough financial situation worshiped God wholeheartedly. So many others, whose stories are too numerous to tell, lifted their voices and their hearts to the One who had redeemed them.

As I saw this happening, I, too, began—albeit, somewhat slowly—to lift my voice in praise to the Lord. As those in close proximity boasted in the Lord, the afflicted—that was me—heard it and began to rejoice. Because they willingly worshiped Him freely, we ended up exalting His name together.

Making the correct choice—worshiping the Lord even in the midst of trying circumstances—really does have an impact on those around us. ❖

Complete Surrender

By the mid 1500s, anyone who publicly acknowledged allegiance to the fledgling protestant movement—and thereby defied the Church of Rome—potentially left themselves open to imprisonment or even death. As the teaching spread, it became increasingly common for people to willingly lose their lives as a result of their newfound faith. Fox's *Book of Martyrs* lists account after account of those people and their stories.

As I recently re-read some of those accounts, one especially struck me. It was the story of five people in England: John Lomas, Agnes Snoth, Anne Wright, Joan Sole, and Joan Catmer. We don't know anything about their positions in this life. We have no idea whether any of them was rich or poor. We are aware that Agnes was a widow and Joan Catmer was married. Of the others, though, we know nothing about their marital status. Fox tells us that John was a "young man," but no ages are given for any of the five. There is not much offered in the way of specifics about them.

Further, they apparently did not have much, if any, connection to one another. They just all happened to be in the same area at the same time. We are also not given any details of the stories surrounding their arrests, except that they were declared to be criminals because of their anti-Roman Catholic beliefs. Fox says only, "These five martyrs suffered together, January 31, 1556."

The story concludes by saying that the five "were burnt at two stakes in one fire, singing hosannahs to the glorified Savior, until the breath of life was extinct."

What a statement! They worshiped their Redeemer until they could no longer do so in this life. However, when this life ended they found themselves in a place where they could worship Him eternally. Thank you, John and Agnes and Anne and both Joans for giving us a great example to follow.

Do you remember the story in the Bible about the lady who poured the perfume on Jesus' feet? "When a woman who had lived a sinful life in that town learned that Jesus was eating at the Pharisee's house, she brought an alabaster jar of perfume, and as she stood behind him at his feet weeping, she began to wet his feet with her tears. Then she wiped them with her hair, kissed them and poured perfume on them." (Luke 7:37-38)

Biblical scholars seem to concur that the alabaster jar of perfume was extremely expensive. Some say it could have cost as much as a year's wages. This was undoubtedly the single most valuable thing she possessed, and she poured it on Jesus' feet! This woman was an extravagant worshiper. She wasn't giving Jesus the leftovers. She apparently offered her very best.

I have been told that adult citizens of Turkey are issued an identification card. It contains all of the personal information about them, much like a driver's license would in the United States. If the person's address or any other information on the card changes, they must get a new card.

There is a major difference, though, between the information on that card and an American driver's license. The Turkish ID card lists the religious affiliation of the carrier. When the card is created, "Muslim" is automatically entered into that space. If their affiliation is different, they have to declare that and have it changed. Of course, if this happens—especially if it changes after the card has already been issued—the person is alienated. Most of the time that person will lose his job. His family disowns him. He will suffer serious persecution. Most Christians are killed.

Some time ago I heard about a group of Turkish refugees who had converted to Christianity. They were temporarily in a neighboring country but soon would be going home. An American missionary noted that during a time of corporate worship, they all held one hand in the air and the other hand at the base of their throat. It was not just one or two who did this; they all worshiped in the same manner. When the missionary inquired about the significance of their actions, he was told that when they returned to Turkey, they would likely be beheaded because of their new-found Christian faith. By worshiping like this they were saying, "Lord Jesus, You're worth dying for."

It's very unlikely that most of us reading this will ever have to face such brutal circumstances. The vast majority of us will not be called to give our lives because of our beliefs. Yet, it seems to me, there is still a lesson we can learn from our Turkish brothers.

For most of us, our worship is more convenient than extravagant. We offer what is easy rather than something of true value. It's no sacrifice to give something that has no significance. But would we—honestly—offer our all? Would we—like the woman with the alabaster jar of perfume—willingly give our very best to Jesus? Could we—even in the face of death, like John and Agnes and Anne and both Joans—still worship our Redeemer? ❖

Worship When You Have To

How do we make the choice to worship—whether we have lost a child, are facing adversity, deprivation, prison, or even death? In the upcoming chapters we'll explore some practical suggestions of how to make this a reality. Sometimes, though, it's merely a choice. We choose to worship even when we don't feel like it. We do it simply because we know it's the right and necessary thing to do. Such is the example of Jenna.

Jenna has known the Lord from a very young age. She was raised in a solid, Christian home, in a very loving atmosphere. Of all her siblings, Jenna is the one with the most creative and artistic bent. She loves to perform—music, acting, mime, dance. She even studied the arts in college. She is a very gifted and talented young woman.

Worshiping the Lord became an increasingly important part of her life, especially as she matured through her college years. In good times and difficult times, Jenna could be found declaring her allegiance to God and receiving His love. In the midst of the congregation or even on her own, she would lavish her love on her Savior. She recalls those intimate times of worship with fond affection.

It was during college that Jenna met Neil. Also a theater major, Neil talked of traveling the world, using the arts as a means of evangelism. Jenna's heart leapt at the possibility of having a partner with whom to do these things. Neil and Jenna had long talks comparing their goals. It seemed like a perfect fit. There was no denying it: they were made for each other. Jenna married Neil with high expectations.

Shortly after they were married, though, something happened. Neil became unsure and changed his mind on some things. He was no longer certain he wanted to take the gospel to other nations through the use of the arts. He really just wanted to remain here in the States. In fact, he told Jenna that their marriage was probably a mistake. A year into their marriage he actually mentioned the possibility of divorce. Jenna felt nauseous. *How could this be happening?* she wondered.

Before marriage, they agreed that they would not be involved in any ministry commitments for at least the first year. Yet, only a few months after the ceremony, Neil was offered a job as a Youth Pastor at a nearby church. Despite Jenna's misgivings, he made the decision to take the position. Neil poured himself into the ministry position, giving Jenna even less time and attention than he had before.

In the midst of this, Jenna was left with a choice. She could continue to attend the church where she had strong mentoring relationships with mature Christians, or she could become part of the church where Neil was now ministering. She left her moorings and followed her husband. Unfortunately, the new church was lifeless. As one who knew acting inside and out, she recognized that for most of the people who attended, Sunday morning services were mostly just a production, an act with little or no life. It wasn't long before Jenna's own spiritual life began to mirror that of the church.

Neil and Jenna continued to be involved in the local theater community, mostly among non-Christians. They had originally talked of being salt and light to the group. In spite of this, Jenna was troubled by Neil's actions in that setting. When they went out as a group, Neil didn't even sit with Jenna. He barely acknowledged her presence. Jenna felt rejected and alone.

As these events unfolded, Jenna struggled. Most of her current friends were non-Christians in the theater group. She was in a church with little—if any—spiritual vitality. Her husband—for all practical purposes—had abandoned her. Jenna didn't realize it, but she had become easy prey.

One of the men in the theater group began to talk with her. It was innocent enough initially. He honestly didn't even realize that Jenna was married. Especially not to Neil. Neil? Who paid her so little attention? What a terrible situation that must be. He offered to talk with Jenna. To listen. To empathize.

The talk was real and honest, not shallow and on the surface. Such conversation was something for which Jenna had longed. It was as though someone had offered a pitcher of ice-water to a person dying of thirst. She drank deeply. It was not the sweetest water she had ever tasted, but it helped quench her thirst—at least for the time. She knew the situation was wrong, but she was so incredibly lonely and so in need of a relationship. It all happened so quickly and so naturally. She certainly never planned to have an affair, but it happened all the same.

Eventually Neil found out about the full extent of the affair. For him, Jenna's infidelity became the way out of a marriage that he regretted. Neil told Jenna he wanted a divorce. In that moment the entire weight of the situation hit her. She felt her heart being ripped from her body. It was like falling into the pitch black darkness of a bottomless pit. It was a blow from which she was sure there could be no recovery. Was she dying? She didn't know for sure. It certainly seemed possible. She did know she needed help. She *really* needed help.

Many of Jenna's Christian "friends" who knew at least part of what had happened turned their backs on her and stopped associating with her. Fortunately, some mature Christian friends from her previous church rescued Jenna. They reached out in love and demonstrated the grace of the Lord Jesus Christ to her. They even gave her a place to live.

Jenna recognized what a mess she had made. She also knew, though, that God was still there, waiting for her. She took the Lord at His Word. "Draw near to God, and he will draw near to you" (James 4:8). She returned to her old church and her former relationships. With the help of others, Jenna was able to take huge steps forward in healing and restoration, but it wasn't easy.

"At first I was going to church because I knew I *needed* to be in church," Jenna told me. "I honestly wasn't sure I even wanted to go. It took an active effort on my part." She said that she was pursuing the Lord because she had to. She knew if she didn't, she would completely die spiritually.

She also admitted that there were difficulties involved. "An unbelievable number of things would come up to keep me from going to church. Car troubles. Sickness. You name it. I got to the point where I just said, 'No! I'm going.' And it was amazing. Each time...*each time* God met me there." On the verge of tears, she paused to regain her composure as she told me her story. "I didn't even necessarily want to be there, yet the Lord touched me *every...single...time.*" Another pause, then a smile. "Then the next week, though, I'd have the same struggles—about not really wanting to go—all over again. I had to force myself, but each time the Lord was faithful to meet me and offer me what I needed most at that point in my life. It was amazing."

Jenna found it exceedingly important to worship in the company of other believers during this time. Because she had felt so alone and abandoned, worshiping among other Christians was needful for her. As Jenna once again began to offer heartfelt worship to God—along with her brothers and sisters in Christ—she once again found the One Who she knew would *never* abandon her.

The Lord restored that intimate worship relationship that she had previously enjoyed. When I asked her if that worship relationship had changed in any way through this ordeal, she gave a profound answer. "No one would probably notice any difference just by looking at me. It's kind of like looking at a lake. On the surface, it looks just like it always has looked. But it is as though someone went beneath the surface and somehow scooped it out and made the lake *much* deeper."

Isn't that just like the Lord? He takes a horrendous situation and uses it to draw us closer to Himself. Somehow He deepens our relationship with Him through our darkest moments.

I've said it before, and I'll say it again. Worship during difficult times is not necessarily easy. Yet, it is still the right thing to do. Sometimes we *choose* to worship long before we *feel* like worshiping. Our worship can offer us a proper perspective about our situation. Once we have that proper perspective, it causes us to worship Him all the more. ❖

Worship Is Not in Opposition to Mourning

As we consider this issue of worshiping God in the dark times, please recognize that I am not suggesting that mourning is wrong. In fact, mourning is very appropriate in many situations. The Bible even tells us that there is "a time to mourn" (Ecclesiastes 3:4). The New Testament encourages us to "weep with those who weep" (Romans 12:15). Sorrow is a legitimate expression.

Pain is real, and sometimes it can hurt a lot. Who can measure the heartache caused by the death of a loved one—or even the loss of a job? I have never known what it is like to wonder from where my next meal would come. I have never experienced the trauma of a life-threatening medical diagnosis or a serious auto-mobile accident. I have not stood and watched as all my earthly possessions were consumed by flames. But I have known people who have experienced such things. And I can tell you honestly that just their descriptions have been heart-wrenching enough. The actual experiences must have been far worse.

God has given us the capacity to mourn and grieve. These things are actually healthy for us. They give us the ability to process pain. They allow us to be honest and give voice to the turmoil within. However, mourning and grieving should not be confused with worship. Nor should such things be seen as a contradiction to worship.

In the opening chapter of the book that bears his name, Job lost nearly everything. All his possessions, his livestock, and even his sons and daughters were all wiped out in a single day. He was left with almost nothing. Yet we are told that Job "fell on the ground and worshiped" (Job 1:20). In the very next verse he declares, "The LORD gave, and the LORD has taken away; blessed be the name of the LORD" (Job 1:21).

Job mourned his losses, but he was not despairing. He grieved, yet he still had hope. Why? Because he knew that even in the midst of tragedy, God was still ruling and reigning. The Lord had not abdicated His throne. Though Job was surely not thrilled with this turn of events, He trusted in His faithful God.

Not long ago my favorite songwriter, Mark Altrogge, penned a new song that caused me to reflect on this whole topic. The song, "As Long as You Are

Glorified," says this:

> Shall I take from Your hand Your blessing,
> yet not welcome any pain?
> Shall I thank You for days of sunshine,
> yet grumble in days of rain?
> Shall I love You in times of plenty,
> then leave You in days of drought?
> Shall I trust when I reap a harvest,
> but when winter winds blow, then doubt?[1]

In the midst of difficulty, in times of tragedy, we experience grief and loss. The pain and the emotional trauma can be excruciating at times. Although such experiences can be overwhelmingly difficult, they should not keep us from worshiping God.

Recently I had the opportunity to meet Cara Brovont. She's a bubbly young Christian mom from Indiana. It didn't take long for me to realize she had quite a story to tell.

Cara first met Derek while they were both waiting in line to see the Christian band, *Jars of Clay*. While waiting for the doors to open, she was eating a pizza and he was hungry. One thing led to another, and the rest, as they say, is history.

Although they initially lived more than two hours apart, when Derek started college near where Cara lived, they began to date. They dated for a couple of years and finally were married. Cara describes Derek as the ideal husband. Caring. Attentive. A strong

Christian walk. She couldn't have asked for more.

Their first daughter, Macie, was born in their first year of marriage. Amie followed two years later. They were happy and content. They bought a house. God had clearly blessed their marriage and family.

One day when Macie was just three years old, her dad came home for lunch. He worked at a research farm and often came home at lunchtime. Derek actually played with Macie during his whole lunch break before heading back to work. As he left, he told Cara that it was going to be a good day, and that he would likely be home by 2:30.

Derek was extremely punctual and very conscientious. When he hadn't arrived home by 3:30, Cara became somewhat concerned but not overly so. It was about an hour later that she got a call from Derek's cell phone. Because they had already used too many minutes that month, Derek had left it lying on his desk. Derek's boss, Travis, was calling to see if she had seen or heard from Derek.

"No," answered Cara. "Is everything okay?"

"Oh, yes," responded Travis. "I'm sure everything is fine."

They hung up, but Travis called back just a few minutes later. "Are you sure you haven't heard from Derek?"

"Yes, I'm sure," replied Cara, wondering what was going on. Unfortunately, Travis had no answers. Cara felt uneasy.

That evening, when Derek still had not arrived home, she went to her mom's house. As Cara approached the house, she noticed a police car parked out front. When she went into the house, her mom was crying. Cara didn't have long to wonder what was going on. An officer stepped across the room toward Cara. He paused and then said, "I'm sorry. There's been an accident. Your husband was killed today."

Every eye in the room was on Cara. No one moved. No one spoke. Cara turned and walked slowly and silently to the bathroom. She went inside and closed the door. Dropping to her knees she said, "Father, God, this is so much bigger than me. I don't really want to do this. I'm 23 years old. I've got two kids. What am I going to do?" She paused, then continued, "Lord, I lay down everything I have. I want my life to be totally what You want it to be. I want You to take over."

As Cara related the story to me, she said, "In that minute I had so much peace. I had no comprehension of what I was going to have to do in the next twenty-four hours, let alone for the rest of my life. But I knew it was going to be okay." God brought to her mind the words of Psalm 28:7, "The Lord is my strength and my shield; my heart trusts in Him, and I am helped; therefore my heart exults, and with my song I shall thank Him" (Psalm 28:7, NASB).

Think about those words for a moment. "My heart exults, and with my song I shall thank Him." Married for less than four years, and now her husband was dead. She was left with two young daughters, one just eight months old. I cannot imagine the grief she experienced in that moment. Yet, in the same moment, she could thank God with her song.

When Cara and I spoke, she repeatedly mentioned how she had seen the faithfulness of God all the way through her ordeal. She was grieving, but she could still recognize that the Lord ruled and reigned. Even in the midst of tragedy—she missed her husband desperately—she could still worship her God.

Because of the context of this book, I asked Cara about her worship life. She responded, "Before Derek passed away I really didn't view worship properly." She told me that afterward she could picture Derek before the throne of God in heaven, worshiping. That image had a profound effect on her own worship life. "Worship has taken on an entirely different dimension."

"Yesterday at church we sang the song, 'Hallelujah, What a Savior.' And I couldn't even sing because I was so caught up in the awesomeness and purity and sovereignty of God. I just stood there and wept as I thought, 'Hallelujah! What a Savior!' Each day I look forward to taking the time to just focus on the Lord and worship Him."

Indeed, what a Savior! Even in the midst of tragedy, even as we grieve a loss or pain, we can still worship that great Savior. He is still worthy.

When your life has been turned upside down—when tragedy has struck at the core of your being—go ahead and mourn. Weep if you need to. Admit the sadness. Voice the grief. All of these are legitimate expressions that God, in His mercy, allows—even encourages—us to utilize. At the same time, though, worship the Lord. Lift your voice in full confidence that the Lord still reigns.

No matter the situation, regardless of the trial, God is still in control and still is deserving of our worship. ❖

Section 2

How to Worship God During the Hard Times

KEY 1
Realize That God Loves You Despite Your Circumstances

Daniel and Christa were raised in very different households. Daniel's parents were loving and attentive; Christa's were distant and aloof. Daniel knew that when he brought home all A's on his report card, his accomplishment would be celebrated. Christa hoped only that her parents might be less harsh when she took first place in the spelling bee. Daniel's parents often let him know that they were proud of his successes. Christa's folks barely acknowledged such achievements.

Yes, those homes were very different, yet in some ways, they were much the same. Daniel recognized early the very disparate reactions he received for his accomplishments compared with his failures. Although his parents celebrated his achievements, they were stern and even harsh when his actions didn't measure up. They provided positive reinforcement when he excelled, but in those moments when he didn't finish in first place, he wondered whether they still loved him.

On the other hand, because her parents never really offered much in the way of affection, Christa never really expected it. Yet, she too noticed the difference between when she did something good and when she did something bad. She may not have received accolades for cleaning her room, but at least for a brief time she wasn't vilified.

Beginning at a very young age, we learn that our value is based on our performance. If we do the right things, if our actions measure up to the set standard, then we have worth. If not, we don't. It's not hard to figure out, especially when the same principles apply in practically every sphere. It makes no difference if we're at home, in school, in social situations, at a job setting, even in church, the rules are the same. The actual standards may vary greatly, but the game is played the same way. Do good and you win; do bad, you lose. Achieve success and you are befriended; fail and no wants to have anything to do with you.

It's no wonder, then, that we carry that same mindset into our relationship with God. When things don't go the way we hope, when a tragic event occurs in our lives, our initial reaction can easily be, "I wonder what I did that caused God to be mad at me."

Have you ever mentioned to friends or coworkers about driving somewhere and encountering all the traffic signals on green? What's the usual response to that scenario? "You must be living right." In other words, the Lord is blessing you because you're doing good.

When things go wrong, though, many of us don't even need to wonder what we've done to arouse God's ire. We know our thoughts and compulsions all too well. In fact, what we've really been wondering is when the proverbial other shoe would drop. After all, how could the Lord possibly love a screw-up like me? Theologically we acknowledge that God does indeed love us, but on the inside we're often held captive by the notion that it's nothing more than wishful thinking. After all, we know the rules of the game, and we don't measure up. Not like those other folks who have their lives in order. God clearly must have greater affection for those people than He does for someone who messes up all the time, right?

Author and teacher Wayne Jacobsen likens this ideology to plucking petals from a daisy. "He loves me. He loves me not." We wonder and stew and ponder and try to figure out if God really loves us by the circumstances we encounter. If things are going well, then, obviously, God loves me. Let difficulty strike, however, and we're sure He has abandoned us. He loves me. He loves me not.

This entire line of thinking strikes right at the very core of the gospel. It puts us back in the mode of needing to measure up. Our drive to achieve—and wondering whether we have achieved enough—nullifies the cross. We end up, in essence, no different from the Muslim family that lives down the road.

The Qur'an lists many different names for God, but love is not one of them. Ask any Muslim if their God loves them and they'll admit they don't know. They hope so. They would certainly like it if he did, but they are unsure if they have done enough to earn his affection. It's Daniel and Christa revisited. And, I might add, it reminds me a whole lot of how you and I often think and act.

Think about this. The Apostle Paul suffered tragedy after tragedy in his life. He was beaten with rods, whipped, shipwrecked, stoned and left for dead. He was mocked and ridiculed. Imprisoned and publicly humiliated. Paul was harassed at nearly every turn.

Based on these events, some would say that the Lord must have been really mad at Paul. After all, why else would so many bad things happen to him? Paul must have been pretty far down on God's list to have experienced so many difficulties. But wait a minute. Consider the whole picture. Was the Lord really mad at Paul?

Paul, the one who wrote the majority of the New Testament letters? Paul, the one who traveled extensively spreading the gospel, starting and strengthening churches throughout the known world? Paul, who had the faith to ignore a venomous, deadly snake that had bitten him? Paul, who regularly stood up to false teachers and denounced heresies? Paul, who in many ways became the point man for the entire New Testament

Church? How could we even begin to suggest that Paul's troubles were because the Lord was upset with him?

We can't *honestly* suggest such a thing. You see, the idea that we as Christians experience troubles because God is mad at us is a wrong premise. It is an erroneous concept that leads to false conclusions. When we believe such a falsehood, then the only possible conclusion in every situation that doesn't go the way we would like is that the Lord is mad. Our troubles must be happening because we've done something to cause it.

Romans 5:6-11 tells us that Christ died for us, justified us and reconciled us to God. He did away with God's wrath. We are no longer enemies; we are His children. He loves us more than we can ever imagine. If you're His child, bad things don't happen as a result of God withholding His love.

The truth is that the Apostle Paul repeatedly worshiped God even in the midst of tragic events. How could he? Because Paul knew God well enough to know that He was completely trustworthy regardless of how the situation appeared.

In his excellent book, *He Loves Me!*, author and teacher Wayne Jacobsen said it like this:

> Imagine if Eve had known God well enough to trust his love for her. How would she have responded to the serpent's charges against God?
>
> I can see her face twisted in wonderment as she tries to hold back her

laughter. "Are you talking about our God? The one who walked with us in the Garden last night and the one who loves us so much he has given us everything for our good? You're saying he would lie to us because he doesn't want us to be like him? Absolutely, totally impossible! Not him. We are his children after all!" And she could have walked away without even a second thought. That's the kind of trust God wants us all to know.[1]

Indeed, that is the kind of trust that the Lord wants us all to know. As we walk through difficult times—confidently trusting Him regardless of the situation—it is much easier to lift our voice and honor our God when we are confident that He loves us. We should, like Job in the Old Testament, confidently declare, "Though He slay me, yet I will trust Him" (Job 1:15).

The Lord has already, in the strongest possible terms, demonstrated His love for us. Jesus' death on the cross shows us clearly that God loves us intensely. "For one will scarcely die for a righteous person—though perhaps for a good person one would dare even to die—but God shows his love for us in that while we were still sinners, Christ died for us" (Romans 5:7-8). In spite of the situations and circumstances that can sometimes seem contrary, the Lord's love toward us is a settled issue. As a result, then, we can make the choice to worship Him regardless of what is happening in or around us. ❖

10

KEY 2
Return to God and His Grace as the Foundation for All We Do

After reading so much about how we should worship God even when life is not going well, there is a chance that you're feeling overwhelmed. You might think, *I know I should do this, but most of the time I don't. I'm a failure.*

Right here, I should, of course, tell you that you're not a failure. That would be the kind, benevolent and politically-correct response. It would be the thing that is expected in our society today. But it would be a lie. The truth is that you are a failure. And so am I. We all are. On our own, we can't do anything of value. We—you and I—fall short of the mark on a regular basis.

That's why Jesus died on the cross for us. It wasn't just for our initial conversion, though. If all His death and resurrection did was to wipe out our sins prior to the day we were first born-again, then we're in an awful lot of trouble. We need His grace and mercy every moment of every day.

You see, the real purpose of the law (all of the do's and don'ts of the Bible) is to push us toward the Lord. "So then, the law was our guardian until Christ came, in order that we might be justified by faith" (Galatians 3:24). The law was, as this verse says in the New International Version, "put in charge to lead us to Christ." The law demonstrates how much we need God and what a mess we are without Him.

Romans 3:20 says basically the same thing: "For by works of the law no human being will be justified in his sight, since through the law comes knowledge of sin." The job of the law is to show us that we are indeed sinners who desperately need God.

Charles Spurgeon said it like this, "The law was a dispensation of terror, which drove men before it as with a scourge; the gospel draws with bands of love... The law repels, the gospel attracts. The law shows the distance which there is between God and man; the gospel bridges that awful chasm, and brings the sinner across it."[1]

It is certainly not difficult to find laws (rules, commandments) from the Bible that we break. For example, "You shall not covet your neighbor's house... or anything that is your neighbor's" (Exodus 20:17).

Have you ever wished you could have something that someone else owns? You've coveted. If you're like most people, you've probably even coveted something recently. Ephesians 4:2 tells us that we should walk with "all humility and gentleness." The word for all here means "full" or "complete." Are you always *completely* humble and gentle? Me neither. When we break the laws of God, we have sinned.

Personally, I welcome the convicting power of the Holy Spirit at work through His Word in my life. You see, I am not just convicted about a bad attitude. Or about an unhealthy fear. Or lewd thoughts. Or a grudge. Or a lust for power. Or covetousness. Or a lack of humility. Oh, to be sure, it may be any or all of these (or a myriad of other things), but first and foremost, I am convicted of sin. Thankfully, I know how to handle sin. I repent and accept God's unmerited grace in the form of Jesus' substitutionary death on the cross.

There is an involuntary reaction that causes us to pull back when we touch something hot. Pain at such times is good. That's what guilt does for us. Without guilt, we do not need grace. The day we lose our consciousness of sin is the day we no longer recognize our need for Christ.

"For you say, I am rich, I have prospered, and I need nothing, not realizing that you are wretched, pitiable, poor, blind, and naked" (Revelation 3:17). These words were not written to unbelievers but to the believers at Laodicea. Jesus had just declared that they were not "cold" but "lukewarm." The problem was not that they were not saved but that they thought they were okay. They were self-righteous. They no longer recognized that they needed God. In the midst of their self-assuredness God calls them "wretched, pitiful, poor, blind and naked."

When we fall short of God's demands—whether it be in worship or any other area of life—there is a remedy: Jesus' death and resurrection. The price has already been paid.

1 John 1:9, tells us, "If we confess our sins, he is faithful and just to forgive us our sins and to cleanse us from all unrighteousness." What a promise! All we have to do is to confess our sins, and God forgives and cleanses us.

So when we find ourselves not worshiping God when we know we should, there's an answer. It is not—as some would suggest—to grit our teeth and do it anyway. There are times when this is necessary, but more often than not we need to repent and ask God to forgive us for our non-worshiping attitude. Then we must recognize that Christ has made a way for us to be forgiven and cleansed and to come before a holy God. It is there—in recognizing the gospel—that we find the power to actually fulfill His commands.

God gives us more than we can bear—on our own

Renowned sports broadcaster Joe Buck is heard nationally on broadcasts of major football and baseball games. Joe is the son of Hall of Fame broadcaster Jack Buck. Jack was the radio voice of the St. Louis

Cardinals for decades. One day when Joe was in his late teens, he was in the Cardinal's broadcast booth with his dad. Joe was not yet a broadcaster; he was just there as a son with his father. At the end of one inning, though, Jack stood up and told Joe the next inning was his. Jack then turned and walked out of the booth. Joe just sat there with his mouth hanging open. Though he had long dreamed of following in his father's footsteps, he wasn't sure he was ready. But by the time the inning began, Joe was ready to go and did a good job. Talk about a baptism by fire!

You know, there are times when God does that to us. He thrusts us into situations for which we are sure we're not prepared, yet just like Jack knew Joe was ready—he had often heard his son doing play-by-play to himself as he sat watching a sporting event—the Lord knows when we're ready. In fact, God knows far better than we do.

The truth, though, is that the Lord offers us a far better situation than Jack did with Joe. God doesn't leave us on our own. He doesn't walk out of the broadcast booth—or whatever the situation might be—and leave us sitting there alone. No, He walks *with us* through each and every situation. He has promised never to leave us (Hebrews 12:5).

Some people say that God will not give us more than we can bear. Actually, as much as I would like to believe that, it's just not true. He does tell us that He will not let us be *tempted* beyond our ability (1 Corinthians 10:13), but that's far different than giving us more than we can bear. Honestly, I think that God regularly gives us more than we can bear so that we have to lean on Him. Our own strength is never going to be enough, so we must rely on His strength (2 Corinthians 12:9-10).

I recently heard a song by Lisa Qualsett and Sue Christensen. The song, entitled "All That Remains," says this:

> If the heat of the trial
> is what will bring the change,
> help me to surrender
> and trust You in the flame.[2]

Whatever your situation, it didn't catch God by surprise.

Perhaps you think your situation is too big or difficult or devastating. Truth be told, if you had to bear it alone, it probably would be too big. Yet the Lord is with you. He has promised to remain with you always.

When your tank is running on empty, the Lord is not only the fuel you need, but He is also the engine itself. Turn to Him. Repent and ask for forgiveness. Then, with confidence placed in Him and His promises, lift your heart and worship. ❖

11
KEY 3
Cultivate an Ongoing Relationship with God Before the Difficult Times

It is clear that even during His visible earthly ministry, Jesus had an extremely close relationship with His Father. He told His disciples, "The Son can do nothing of his own accord, but only what he sees the Father doing. For whatever the Father does, that the Son does likewise" (John 5:19). Luke 5:16 tells us that Jesus took time aside (in "lonely places") and prayed. The Greek phrasing in this verse has the connotation of this happening frequently. Jesus so pursued a close, intimate relationship with the Father, that He was ultimately totally dependent on Him. There was no separating the two.

Of course, as Christians, we too have a relationship with the Father. Because of what Jesus has done for us on the cross, we have become a part of His family. We are, because of Christ's atoning sacrifice, related to the Father. We can call Him Daddy, because He has adopted us into His family.

At the same time, though, there is more to true relationship than simply being a part of the same family. My children are a part of my family. They are, in every sense of the word, related to me. But that's different than *relationship*.

Some years ago, I saw a movie where a man kidnapped a woman. He loved her and wanted her to love him. But she really didn't care for him at all. So he thought that if he took her away and kept her for himself, she would eventually change her mind and fall for him. In an attempt to make that happen he took her to a cabin in a very remote area. It was just the two of them with no one else for miles around. It was an interesting idea he had to get her to love him. The trouble was that her every waking moment was spent trying to figure out how to escape from the maniac. Not exactly conducive to building a relationship, is it?

Over the years I have pursued a relationship with my kids. I have sat and talked with them. I have spent time with them, attending events that were important and meaningful in their lives. I have shared some of my hopes and my core beliefs with them. I have taken them on trips, prayed with them, hugged them, and shared words of affirmation with them. All of these things and more have been, at least in part, an attempt to build relationship with them. But if they refuse all of my advances, there ultimately will be no relationship. If they are not interested in having a real, honest, true relationship with me, I cannot force them to do it. Relationships just don't work that way. We would still be related, but the relation*ship* would be nonexistent.

In the same way, God offers us a relationship with Himself. Many people have accepted the Lord's forgiveness and are, therefore, born-again into the family of God. They are related to the Father. But that's different than having an actual relationship with Him.

That is why Jesus pursued such an intimate relationship with His Father. In good times and bad, Jesus trusted His Father completely. There was no room for wondering or doubting in Jesus' mind. Why? Because He knew His Father too well to even consider such things.

Even when Jesus had to endure the struggle of Calvary, He continued to look to His Father. Oh, there was agony. The pain was real. Being abandoned by His closest earthly friends must have been traumatic—the whipping and mocking, the piercing of the flesh by those cruel spikes. Undoubtedly, it was agonizing.

I think the movie, *The Passion of the Christ* portrays the entire scenario well. I could barely watch the movie. More than the mental trauma, the horrendous physical torture that Jesus endured must have been horrific. But He endured because His eyes were locked on His Father. He had a relationship with the Ever-Present One, and that sustained Him even through those long, pain-filled hours.

What would have happened if Jesus knew His Father, yet waited to develop a real, honest, intimate relationship with Him until the night He was arrested? Would such a relationship have sustained Him during those dark hours? Of course not.

Author and poet Evelyn Gunter wrote some amazing and thought-provoking words:

> A cold November wind blew lazy snowflakes across the cemetery. I pulled the coat around me more tightly as I stood by a new mound. Summer flowers had been hardened by the frost. I knelt beside them with a sense of gratitude.
>
> "Thank you, Lord," I whispered. "Thank you for my family in heaven." I looked over at Baby Samuel's small white stone. He was the first of the family to enter heaven.
>
> Then my attention came back to the nearest grave, unmarked as yet. It was the final resting place for my minister husband. The fresh sod, soon to be covered by snow, suggested hope, not despair. I was thankful, for I knew the second member of my family had been called into the presence of the Lord. A warmth filled my heart as I realized they were with Jesus, waiting to welcome me

when my task would be done. I had a
new sense of rejoicing in the Blessed
Hope.[1]

Doesn't this scenario sound at least a bit odd to
our ears? Rejoicing in a cemetery? Thanking God while
kneeling beside the grave of a recently departed spouse?
From a non-Christian perspective, this idea is ludicrous.

Yet, it is clear that Evelyn Gunter knew her God.
She was able to kneel beside those graves and give thanks
because she *knew* the Lord and the truth of His promises.
The untimely deaths of her son and her husband could not
be compared with her relationship with Jesus.

Toward the end of the Old Testament book that
bears his name, Job reminisces about when "I was in my
prime, when the friendship of God was upon my tent..."
(Job 29:4). Job remembered the closeness of his relationship with the Lord. Is that why Job could worship
when everything was taken away? Was it because he
had known, as the NIV says, "God's intimate friendship," that Job could worship in the midst of tragedy?

I came into a saving relationship with the Lord
Jesus Christ when I was in high school. Some of the first
books I read after being born-again taught me the importance of praising God in the good times and the bad. After
all, 1 Thessalonians 5:18 tells us to "give thanks in all circumstances." Books like *Prison to Praise* and *Let Us
Praise* helped solidify in my mind the idea that the Lord
was worthy, regardless of the situation. The truth, though,
is that although those books taught me the importance of

praising God even during difficult times, I don't recall them telling me how to do it.

Would you like to be able to worship God, even in the midst of difficulty? Here's one of the primary keys: Develop a relationship with the Father now. Waiting until you're in the midst of some traumatic event will be too late.

The Lord is pursuing you now. Don't push Him aside. Seek Him. Read His Word. Pray. Fellowship with the other members of His Body here on earth. If you know Him—I mean really know Him—then worshiping Him during difficult times will be far easier. When we learn to trust Him day by day with the ordinary situations of life, then we'll know His faithfulness and can trust Him in the dark times also. ❖

12

KEY 4
Recognize that a Godly Life Is Not a Trouble-Free Life

Our society—the Church included—has bought into a lie. It is not a mean-faced, ugly lie. We don't shrink back from it when this lie is spoken. It does not appear to be a world-domination type of lie that keeps people awake at night. It is, in fact, a feel-good lie. If we believe it, it can help us to have pleasant thoughts and dreams. This lie can potentially cause us to be less worried and anxious about our lives than we might be otherwise. However, this lie is as sinister and destructive as any lie that hell ever secreted into the minds of mankind.

What is this terrible lie that we have believed? It is simply this: A good life is one that is free from trouble. As a Christian, I should expect to have a good life.

"Hold on a minute, Tom. I don't believe that."

No? Then tell me this: How do you react when things don't go your way? What type of thoughts run through your mind when trials and difficulties come at you? Do you have the same reaction to such events as when you get a promotion on your job? Or when your child makes the team? Or when you drive off the lot in that new car? Do you?

Okay, probably not. Trying times are not nearly as much fun as those other events, are they? We will most likely never have an excited reaction to difficulties, yet neither should we have a despairing reaction to them.

Somehow don't we hope that living to please God will exempt us from the difficulties? It is hard, though necessary, to admit that the New Testament predicts that Christ's followers will have troubles.

You see, if we truly believe that hard times are to be expected in this life, then we won't react to them with such a woe-is-me attitude. We will talk soon about how recognizing the reality of heaven can change our perception of facing difficult times, but so can understanding that difficult times are simply a natural part of life here on earth.

As much as we would prefer to deny it, the fact is that everything in this life won't always go our way. There will be events that will tax us to our limits. We will face trials and difficulties that will stretch us beyond what we think we can endure.

So when those events take place, we can view

them as horrendous oddities—something that is clearly not an acceptable part of this life—or we can recognize that, like it or not, difficult times occur in every life. Always have, always will.

"Beloved, do not be surprised at the fiery trial when it comes upon you to test you, as though something strange were happening to you" (1 Peter 4:12). This verse certainly makes it sound as though hard times should be viewed as a usual, even expected, part of our lives. Clearly, God's Word declares that "fiery trials" are not "something strange." They are simply a part of life.

Someone once said that difficulties in life are like thorns on roses: You can't get the rose without the thorns. It's all part of the same package.

I remember Sunday School lessons from my childhood. Each week we heard the exciting stories of the Bible. Daniel surviving through the night in a den of hungry lions. The miraculous deliverance of the Israelites from slavery in Egypt. Three friends— Shadrach, Meshach and Abednego—entering a blazing furnace and coming out alive. Elijah confronting the prophets of Baal on Mount Carmel and the resulting revival. The shepherd boy, David, killing a mighty warrior-giant with just a sling and a stone. Elisha single-handedly capturing the Syrian army as the Lord struck the Syrians blind. Even now I still find the thrill of such stories awe-inspiring. The best part is that they are true.

Although my Sunday School adventures are now long past, these stories still serve as the basis for many Sunday School classes today. Such faith-building stories can create a good foundation for trusting in God. However, when we have a steady diet of *only* such stories, the result can be a distorted perspective of life here on earth.

Honestly, I think that some people who teach from the Bible either miss many of the details or they purposely leave out those details because such things are inconvenient. For example, over the years I have heard many sermons based on Hebrews 11, the great faith chapter of the Bible. This recounting of heroes is a veritable Who's Who list, a Hall of Fame from throughout the pages of Scripture. Yet some of the final verses of that same chapter are rarely held up as the same shining example as the earlier verses.

> Some were tortured, refusing to accept release, so that they might rise again to a better life. Others suffered mocking and flogging, and even chains and imprisonment. They were stoned, they were sawn in two, they were killed with the sword. They went about in skins of sheep and goats, destitute, afflicted, mistreated—of whom the world was not worthy—wandering about in deserts and mountains, and in dens and caves of the earth (Hebrews 11:35-38).

As I recently reread those verses, I wasn't sure I would have enjoyed being one of those people.

Tortured. Flogged. Imprisoned. Stoned. Sawn in two. Killed with the sword. Destitute. Mistreated. These are not the things of happy stories. Maybe that's why we tend to skip over such passages.

There are, of course, lots of other details that are omitted from many people's teaching of the Bible. Although we are enamored with the shepherd boy turned king, we can easily forget that a man named Uriah was cut down in the prime of his life—murdered in cold blood—because of David's lust. Every child in Sunday School celebrates David's victory over Goliath. Yet, the story about David passing through the Valley of Elah—the very place where he slew Goliath—years later under very different circumstances, is often omitted. David was running for his life from Saul and was on his way to seek refuge from the Philistines where he would feign insanity just to survive.

We are thrilled with the mercy of God that turned the Church's most ardent persecutor into its greatest preacher and theologian. However, we miss the fact that it was apparently more than ten years from the time that God rescued Saul of Tarsus from his wayward path until Saul—turned Paul—began his ministry.

Sunday School lessons celebrate the ultimate ascent of Joseph to second in command in Egypt. Yet, his being sold into slavery by his own brothers and then wrongly accused and put in prison, apparently for years, are given only minimal mention in this epic drama.

We love the miraculous rescue of the Israelites from Egypt, yet we often ignore a couple of very important facts: they wandered in the desert for *forty years* and almost no one who left Egypt actually entered the Promised Land.

So what's the point of bringing up such often-ignored details? In the midst of the thrilling, positive stories of Scripture, there is also heartache, struggle, waiting, disappointment and difficulty. If we focus *only* on the miracles and excitement, we can end up with a skewed picture of life in at least two ways.

First, we can easily begin to think that each moment of every day should be filled with grand and glorious events, full of wonder, excitement and adventure. Let's be honest, though. That's not really what life is like. In fact, it's not even what life is *supposed to* be like. Think about it for a moment. If God expected every moment of each day to be a thrilling adventure, then why does the Bible speak so much about things like perseverance, diligence, patience and faithfulness? The answer should be obvious. The everyday, mundane tasks are a large part of real life.

Second, such a picture of life depicts only the positive and not the negative. Here's the sad part: like it or not, there are negative aspects of life. Oh, it certainly was not part of the original design, but sin changed that design. So until that final, glorious day when Jesus visibly returns, we have to deal with the effects of sin in the world. Not just our own sin, but sin in general. Those effects include realities such as suffering, waiting and difficult situations.

Unfortunately, no one is immune from such

effects. No amount of money—and no amount of sanctification—will ward off the consequences of mankind's fallenness. Walking with the Lord longer than someone else does not exempt you from going through struggles and hardships. Reading your Bible more, or praying more frequently, or worshiping God more often will not negate the possibility of broken relationships and heartache. These things are part of life here on earth.

Let's be clear on this. We should, in fact, teach the positive. People need to see the God-at-work-in-everyday-life stories from Scripture. However, we must also instill in people that at least part of life is mundane, and that we will have difficulties. Otherwise, when people experience such things, they begin to think it is something out of the ordinary, when, in fact, it is not out of the ordinary at all.

As I write this, I have been going through a week of patience-building. Don't you love those times in your own life? I won't give you all the gory details of mine, just a couple of highlights. It began with a computer hard-drive crash early in the week (and all the fun times that accompany such an event in the ensuing days) and finally culminated in a five-hour flight delay at the end of the week. After being delayed for so long, when I finally went through security, I was informed that their computer had randomly chosen me for additional screening. I laughed and thanked God. By that point, being inconvenienced was becoming normal. After all of the other things I had experienced throughout the week, this was no big deal.

I should probably confess that my reaction to the hard-drive crash wasn't quite the same. In many ways, my attitude stunk at that point. You see, it is easier to thank and praise God during difficult times, when difficult times are recognized as a normal part of life. When we view such things as unusual and out of the ordinary—or, worse yet, as an indication that God is mad at us—then worship becomes arduous, not a natural response. On the other hand, when we understand that trials are a normal, even expected, part of life, then we are more likely to turn to God in worship when we encounter them.

Some years ago I heard about a woman who was born in the early eighteen-hundreds. At just six weeks of age she developed a cold. The cold, in turn, caused an inflammation around her eyes. The family called for the doctor, but he was out of town. Instead, another man posing as a doctor made the call. He checked the girl and prescribed a treatment of hot poultices for her eyes. The ingredients in the poultices coupled with the high temperatures caused irreversible damage to the infant's eyes. She was blind for the rest of her life.

That incident alone would have been enough tragedy for one life, but there was more. Her father died when she was only one year old. Much later, after she married, her only child died in infancy.

Imagine such a life, if you will. An imposter posing as a physician caused her to lose her sight. Such a tragedy could certainly cause one to harbor bitterness. Her father was wrenched from her before she even really had a chance to know him. Then, a tragedy of unimaginable proportions: her own dear child died shortly after being born. Still later, she lived through what is arguably the most tragic time in the history of our nation: the Civil War. She did not just live through it, but did so as a sightless person. Were there terrors that she encountered because of her blindness that others never had to bear? We don't know for sure, but it is certainly probable.

Wouldn't it be likely that such a person could easily have become bitter? Wouldn't it, in fact, seem normal to us that she would turn against God and give up all hope? She easily could have felt cheated in life. No one would have blamed her if she had become a resentful and even cynical woman.

But she didn't. No, in fact she became a woman of extraordinary worship.

The average hymnal contains a little over six-hundred hymns. Take a dozen such hymnals and stack them up, and that would still not equal the number of hymns Fanny Crosby—the blind lady—wrote during her lifetime.

> Thou my everlasting Portion,
>> more than friend or life to me,
> All along my pilgrim journey,
>> Savior, let me walk with Thee.
> Not for ease or worldly pleasure,
>> nor for fame my prayer shall be;
> Gladly will I toil and suffer,

only let me walk with Thee.
Close to Thee, close to Thee...
Gladly will I toil and suffer,
    only let me walk with Thee.[1]

If those words were written by someone whose life had been one of ease, they would be shallow and lifeless. To say, "I will toil and suffer," and yet never know the real meaning of suffering, would ring hollow. But if one whose life had been filled with difficulty—one who did not have a carefree existence—wrote such words, then those words would take on far more meaning, and so they do.

Fanny confided to friends that if her sight had remained intact throughout her lifetime, she might have been too easily distracted by all the beautiful things around her to use her mind as fully as she did. She actually thanked God that she had lost her ability to see. "Darkness may throw a shadow over my outer vision," declared Fanny, "but there is no cloud that can keep the sunlight of hope from a trustful soul."[2]

Fanny Crosby wrote so many hymns, it is difficult to choose only a few to share here. Let me offer just one more small section from one of them.

Praise the Lord, praise the Lord,
Let the earth hear His voice!
Praise the Lord, praise the Lord,
Let the people rejoice!
O come to the Father, through Jesus the Son,

And give Him the glory,
great things He has done.[3]

Are these the words of a bitter person? Could a person who had succumbed to the tragedies of life declare such words of praise? No. These are words of praise for a God who has been faithful even in the midst of difficulties.

Recognize that difficult times are simply a part of life. Don't be undone by them. They are not unusual. Instead, as you face such times, choose to worship God. ❖

13
KEY 5
Recognize that God Is Still in Control Regardless of the Situation

One big step that will help us more readily worship God in the hard times is to recognize His sovereignty. When we know that the Lord is at work regardless of how the situation appears on the surface, it becomes easier to trust Him, and therefore to worship Him.

"And we know that for those who love God all things work together for good, for those who are called according to his purpose" (Romans 8:28). I find this statement amazing. "All things work together for good." Somehow the Lord takes everything that happens in the lives of His people and makes those things work for good. The situation itself may not be good, but God will ultimately cause it to work together for good.

Certainly, I don't always recognize it when this is happening in my own life. Many things have occurred to me that have caused me to question this verse. In the lives of other saints I have witnessed apparent devastation—debilitating illness, job loss, divorce, and more—and wondered how God could possibly cause such things to work together for good. Yet He does. Oh, it is not always obvious on the surface. Sometimes we never figure it out during our days here on earth. At the same time, though, the Lord is always faithful and true to His Word.

As I recently reread the story of Ruth in the Old Testament, I saw the truth of this verse again. It was not so much God's work in the life of Ruth that struck me, but His working in the life of Naomi, her mother-in-law.

Naomi was an Israelite, but had moved with her husband and two sons to Moab because of a famine. Naomi's husband died while they were living in this foreign land. The two sons married, but, some years later, they too died. Naomi's entire blood-related family was gone, so she decided to return to Israel.

Both of her daughters-in-law wanted to go with her, but she tried to dissuade them from going. One finally relented and stayed, but the other, Ruth, went with her. When they arrived back in Israel, people in the town recognized Naomi. They welcomed her, but she told them not to call her Naomi (which means "pleasant"), but instead to call her Mara (which means "bitter").

Naomi was obviously not happy. She was mad at God. "The Almighty has dealt very bitterly with me," she said. Naomi could not see any good in this situation at all. None.

Yet, what happened? Ruth ended up marrying Boaz. Their firstborn child was the grandfather of King David, and part of the lineage of Jesus, the Savior. God worked through this apparent devastation—the death of Naomi's husband and two sons—in order to bring good. Don't misunderstand. I'm not suggesting that the Lord *caused* the situation, only that He ultimately used it. Naomi didn't recognize it, but God still worked in and through that situation.

Earlier in the Old Testament, Joseph was sold into slavery by his brothers. That must have been a harrowing experience. Ultimately, though, he became second-in-command of the nation of Egypt and ended up rescuing the nation—and his family—from famine. His trip to Pharaoh's right hand was filled with heartache, pain and even betrayal, yet God somehow worked His plan. Although Joseph did not necessarily see the Lord's hand each step of the way, it was still there.

Like Joseph in the Old Testament, we can't always understand at the time the things that happen. They often don't make any sense. Still, God works in and through those situations, just like He did for Joseph.

Here's the truth: In order to really worship in hard times we must believe that God is working even when we don't see how.

I have come to a point in my life where I realize that all the things that *seem* bad ain't necessarily so. Further, all the things that *seem* good ain't neither.

(Sorry for the grammar infractions, but they seemed appropriate.)

Some time ago I heard an amazing illustration of this truth. Since early childhood, a Christian young woman had dreamed of ministering in India. She loved the country, she loved the people, and she had a burning desire to go as a missionary and share her faith in Christ Jesus with them.

She worked and studied, preparing for ministry in India. After a lengthy time of preparation, the Mission Board of her church accepted her application as a missionary, and she was on her way. She packed up all her worldly belongings and she was officially sent to India as a missionary. Her lifelong dream was finally being fulfilled.

Shortly after arriving in India, though, she received word that her sister and brother-in-law were killed in an accident. That would have been tragedy enough. With her recent move it was unlikely that she would even be able to attend the funerals. To compound the misfortune, she was asked to come back home and care for their three orphaned children.

What a dilemma! She had just begun to see the fulfillment of her goal as a missionary in India. After all the work and study and preparation, how could she just give it all up? Yet she knew in her heart it was the right thing to do. So, leaving the land that she loved so dearly, she once again packed her belongings and returned home to become mother to three grieving youngsters.

And mother she became. She loved those kids as

though they were her own. In big and small ways she consistently demonstrated her care for them. As a result, they began to reciprocate and love her back. Moreover, because of her undeniable love for the Savior, they too began to love Him. And because of her obvious passion for India and its people, the three of them also developed a passion for her beloved India.

Here's the amazing twist. Today, all three of those children are married adults with children of their own, and guess what. Each of them serves as a missionary to India.

There is no way the woman could have envisioned such a scenario when she packed up her possessions that second time to head home. It must have seemed like her world was crumbling. It certainly could have appeared as though God had abandoned her, but He hadn't. He was at work behind the scenes in His own mysterious way.

There is an overarching truth in all of this. We have a hope that ultimately God will work in and through each and every one of our situations for our good and His glory. We don't necessarily always see the good—sometimes, but not always—but it is there just the same. God never fails.

I recently had the privilege of preaching at Oleviste Church in Tallinn, the capital of Estonia. The church building is a huge, ancient cathedral. The first mention of it in historical records was from the thirteenth century. No one is quite sure exactly when the building was actually constructed.

The retired pastor shared a bit of the history of the church after the Sunday services. He said that when the communists were firmly in control of Estonia, they wanted to put an end to the Christian churches in Tallinn. Rather than just shutting them down, however, the communists decided to get the churches to destroy themselves. They confiscated the buildings where each church met and told them they could still meet, but they would now have to meet together in this ancient cathedral that was sitting empty and in disrepair. Evangelical Christians, Baptists, Free Evangelicals, Pentecostals and others were forced to work together. The communists were sure that the theological differences—many were quite significant—would cause the churches to fight one another and ultimately destroy each other.

The plan didn't work, though. Instead, the churches began to willingly work together. They united around the things they could clearly agree on—the basic tenets of the faith—and rather than breaking apart, the church began to grow. In fact, some years later there was such a monumental revival in the church that it impacted hundreds of thousands of people—perhaps millions—all over the Eastern Bloc. People were born-again and many were physically healed in miraculous ways. All this happened under—and much to the dismay of—the communist regime.

Although the original prognosis looked bleak, God worked in and through that situation. Somehow, even in the midst of unlikely and seemingly dire circumstances, the Lord's hand is still active.

Jesus demonstrated this principle so well from the cross. Just after asking His Father why He had forsaken Him, Jesus confidently declared, "Father, into your hands I commit my spirit." (Luke 23:46). He couldn't see His Father in that situation, yet He trusted Him just the same.

Remember Paul, the apostle, in the Philippian jail? The church that was started there when the jailer got saved helped to fund Paul's journeys elsewhere. The Lord somehow used that bad situation for good.

For the mother at the hospital with her child fighting cancer, perhaps God led them to cross paths with doctors, nurses and fellow patients who needed to know of the life-giving Spirit of God who lives in them. It wasn't like they planned to have a hospital ministry, yet God can somehow weave His plan into that scenario.

There is nothing too horrendous for the Lord to redeem. No life has gone too far. No situation is too terrible that God cannot cause it to work for good. Will you trust that He is at work even in those situations and circumstances you don't understand?

God *is* at work. We may not always see it, yet if we trust His faithfulness, we can still worship Him in the midst of tragedy. Into His hands we can commit our lives. ❖

KEY 6A
Understand True Joy

The sixteenth verse of 1 Thessalonians 5 is one of the shortest verses in the Bible. It contains just two words. Without looking it up in your Bible, which one of these do you think is really 1 Thessalonians 5:16?

a. Rejoice sometimes
b. Rejoice occasionally
c. Rejoice always

If you chose "c" then you pass the pop quiz. Nice job.

Okay, it was pretty easy to figure out. Somehow

we can't imagine God telling us to rejoice only now and then. Yet, let's be totally honest for a moment: do you *always* rejoice? Yeah, I didn't think so.

The truth is that most people struggle with the concept of rejoicing, at least occasionally. Oh, we can rejoice when things are going well, but it's a lot more difficult when the winds of adversity are blowing.

Now, before I go too far here and assume that everyone has a certain level of knowledge of language, let me clarify something. The word "rejoice" is the verb form of joy. We could do a comparative analogy like when we were in junior high school: *Rejoice* is to *joy* as *sing* is to *song*. Just like we sing songs, we rejoice joy. Joy is expressed through rejoicing. So when the Bible tells us to rejoice, it means we're to express joy. The joy that is on the inside comes to the surface through rejoicing. I thought it would be best to explain that right off the bat, since I'll be using both of those words quite extensively throughout this chapter. Okay, with that bit of housekeeping taken care of, let's continue.

Acts 13:50-52 tells the story of Paul and Barnabas preaching in the region of Antioch. Scripture says: "But the Jews incited the devout women of high standing and the leading men of the city, stirred up persecution against Paul and Barnabas, and drove them out of their district. But they shook off the dust from their feet against them and went to Iconium. And the disciples were..." The next few words in this passage tell the disciples' reaction to this situation.

Try to imagine this scene. Paul and Barnabas

were preaching the good news about Jesus and they get booted out of the city. So how do you think they should react? What would you do? I have to wonder how I might react in such a situation. Perhaps the next phrase should tell us that the disciples were "disgusted with the whole thing." That would be a typical reaction, wouldn't it?

That is not, however, what happened. The Bible tells us that the disciples were "...filled with joy and with the Holy Spirit." Excuse me?! They were forcibly removed from the city, and they were "filled with joy..."? Unfortunately, that's not our usual response to such difficulties.

In 2 Corinthians 6:4 and following, Paul paints a bleak-looking picture of his life as a Christian. He speaks of "afflictions, hardships, calamities, beatings, imprisonments, riots, labors, sleepless nights, hunger." He mentions being slandered, dishonored, treated as an imposter, punished and more. Paul has definitely not had an easy go of life. Toward the end of this dire-sounding description, Paul makes a statement that almost seems out of context with the rest. He says that he is "sorrowful, *yet always rejoicing...*" (2 Corinthians 6:10, author's emphasis). One translation phrases it slightly differently: "We know sorrow, yet our joy is inextinguishable." *Inextinguishable.* You can't put it out! I love that!

Most people in the church today cannot even begin to relate to the depth of trouble and sorrow the apostle Paul knew. He was whipped five times (39 lashes each time) by his own countrymen. He was beaten with rods three times and stoned and left for dead once.

Paul was shipwrecked three times and even spent a night and a day in the open sea. Yet, in spite of all of these circumstances he still says, "We know sorrow, yet our joy is *inextinguishable.*" What an amazing statement!

It seems to me that—in light of Paul's statement—most of us in the Church today have not yet fully understood this thing called joy.

James adds these thoughts to the scriptural concept of joy: "Consider it *pure joy*, my brothers, whenever you face trials of many kinds..." (James 1:2 NIV, author's emphasis). In this context, what does the word "pure" mean? Whenever I've asked this question in a public setting, some of the answers I commonly receive include, "unadulterated" and "the real essence." James is saying that this is the type of joy we should have—unadulterated, the real essence, pure—whenever we face trials.

Forgive me for meddling but is that *your* normal reaction to trials? Do you consider difficult, troublesome situations in your life to be joy-filled? If not, then perhaps you're missing something. Maybe joy isn't what we always thought it was.

It's been nearly two decades since Clarence Thomas faced weeks of arduous congressional hearings which ultimately resulted in his being approved as a Supreme Court judge. The hearings were particularly trying because he had some very stiff opposition from certain members of congress. Because of the strong antagonism, at one point during the hearing he bowed his head, and, in his deep voice, said, "Since this process began, there has not been one day of joy, there has not been one hour of joy, there has not been one moment of joy." In saying this I believe that Clarence Thomas—just like most of the rest of the world—missed the true, biblical understanding of joy. Unfortunately, much of the Church has taken their cues from the world and has also missed real, godly joy.

Our society tries to tell us that joy comes from doing what makes you feel good; the things that bring momentary happiness are full of joy. Drugs, sex, alcohol—all filled with the fleeting rush of excitement—are examples of this type of ideology. However, if this way of thinking were true, then the chronic alcoholic and the hopeless drug addict would be the most joyful people on earth. Obviously this is erroneous. Joy does not come from things or sensations. True joy is a by-product of the victory won by Jesus on the cross. And nothing, real or imagined, can take it from us without our permission.

The problem that we encounter is that we confuse joy with happiness. Although in one sense joy and happiness are similar, they are not synonymous. Joy is broader and deeper.

The word "happiness" comes from the same root as "happening." The root is an old English word, "hap," that means luck. Maybe you are familiar with another old English word, "happenstance"—circumstances that come to you by luck.

The idea of happiness, then, has to do with circumstances in life being positive:

- Traffic was not bad on my way to work

today, so I'm happy.
- I received an unexpected gift, so I'm happy.
- The kids behaved today, so I'm *really* happy.

All of these are examples of happiness, not joy. Joy is deeper. It is a gift from God. External circumstances cannot affect it without you allowing them to affect it.

Romans 14:17 says: "For the kingdom of God is not a matter of eating and drinking, but of righteousness, peace and joy in the Holy Spirit." Let's examine this passage closely. The kingdom of God is not something we can conjure up on our own. It is something only God can bring about. Similarly, the components of the kingdom that are listed are also gifts from Him.

Righteousness—Righteousness does not come from deciding to be righteous. We have been made righteous by the blood of Jesus (Titus 3:5). It is a gift.
Peace—We cannot find peace by making a decision to have peace. Jesus said, "Peace I leave with you; my peace I give you" (John 14:27). Again, it is a gift.
Joy—In the same way, joy does not come from trying to have more joy. Paul told the church at Thessalonica, "...in spite of severe suffering, you welcomed

the message with the *joy given by the Holy Spirit*" (1 Thessalonians 1:6, author's emphasis). Joy, too, is a gift.

A similar message is conveyed in the sixteenth chapter of Acts. Paul and Silas were in prison when there was such a strong earthquake that the doors of the prison flew open and everyone's chains were loosed. Under Roman law, if prisoners escaped, the life of the one guarding the prisoners was forfeit, so the jailer was about to kill himself because he was sure that everyone had escaped. Paul, however, called out to him and told him that the prisoners were all still there. When Paul shared the good news about Jesus with the jailer, he and his family were born again. This section continues by telling us that the jailer was "*filled with joy* because he had come to believe in God" (Acts 16:34, NIV, author's emphasis). The Lord gave him the gift of joy when he was converted.

Joy cannot be generated by us. Only God can give it and if you're a believer in Jesus, He already has.

Joy Is Not a Side Issue

Many believers don't view joy as a very important subject. They suppose we should probably hear a sermon about it once every ten years or so, but that's probably enough. After all, it really isn't all that important of a topic, is it?

Actually, joy holds a prominent place in Scripture. The Greek word for "joy" is found 61 times in the New Testament. The Greek word for "rejoicing" is used 78 times in the New Testament. This concept of joy, then, is found *139 times* in the New Testament. Obviously this is not a side issue. It is something that we as the Church should understand more fully than we have in the past.

When the biblical writers wanted to emphasize a point, they did not have the various typesetting tools that we have available today. When I write, if I want to emphasize something I can use **bold-face** or *italics* to cause it to stand out. As we read, we know that we should pay special attention to such things. In the early Hebrew culture these tools were not available. Instead, to emphasize a point, they used a simple literary device: repetition. If they wanted to demonstrate that something they were saying was really, really important, they would repeat it for emphasis.

A good example of this is found in the sixth chapter of Isaiah. The six-winged seraphs were calling to one another about the Lord. Remember their words? "Holy, holy, holy is the LORD of hosts..." (Isaiah 6:3). It was not enough for them to say that God was "Holy." It was apparently not even adequate to describe Him as "Holy, holy." The Lord's holiness needed to be strongly emphasized so it was stated and then repeated two more times.

The apostle Paul used this emphasis-giving repetition in his writings also. In his letter to the Philippian church he said, "Finally, my brothers, rejoice in the Lord! It is no trouble for me to write the same things to you again, and it is a safeguard for you" (Philippians

3:1). Later in the same letter he repeats this concept: "Rejoice in the Lord always. I will say it again: Rejoice!" (Philippians 4:4).

In essence Paul is saying: "This joy thing is so important—I want you to get it. Rejoice in the Lord! Don't miss this. Express the joy God has given you!" He repeated it several times to make certain they understood the significance of what he was saying. We, too, would do well to heed his words. Rejoicing—releasing the joy that is already resident within us—is essential for our lives as Christians.

Tim Hansel is a respected teacher and author in the Body of Christ. In his book, *You Gotta Keep Dancin'*, Tim shares about a life-changing experience he had. While climbing a mountain he fell off a high cliff. As his climbing partner watched in horror, Tim landed flat on his back far below. The intense blow injured his spine far more than he immediately realized. Although he is able to walk and do most of the things he was capable of before, Tim has lived for over thirty years in nearly-constant pain. Despite his injury, he says this:

> Pain is inevitable but misery is optional. We cannot avoid pain, but we can avoid joy. God has given us such immense freedom that He will allow us to be as miserable as we want to be.
>
> I know some people who spend their entire lives practicing being unhappy, diligently pursuing joylessness. They

get more mileage from having people
feel sorry for them than from choosing to
live out their lives in the context of joy.[1]

Perhaps you know someone like that. I have met several people over the years who would much rather lament even the minor inconveniences of life than to be joyful in spite of those situations.

In the fifth chapter of Acts, Peter and other apostles had been healing people in the Name of Jesus and winning many converts. The Sadducees were jealous of them and had them arrested. That night an angel set the apostles free and told them to continue preaching. The following day they were brought before the Sanhedrin. The strong words of Peter and the others caused the members of the Sanhedrin to become furious. They wanted to have the apostles killed.

Finally, Gamaliel, a teacher of the law who was respected by all the people, addressed the Sanhedrin. "So they took his advice, and when they had called in the apostles, they beat them and charged them not to speak in the name of Jesus, and let them go" (Acts 5:40). At that point most Christians in our culture would be irate. After all, they had been thrown in jail for spreading the good news. Sure, they were let out of jail by an angel, but they were rearrested the next day. Then they were flogged and told to stop preaching. "Hey," we would probably think, "this is getting a little too rough." We would likely whine and complain to anyone who would listen, wouldn't we?

The entire scenario apparently didn't even faze the apostles. They still maintained their joy through the whole situation: "Then they left the presence of the council, *rejoicing* that they were counted worthy to suffer dishonor for the name" (Acts 5:41, author's emphasis). Rejoicing?! I thought they had just been flogged and rebuked publicly. Is it possible that we could learn from this story?

Later, while writing, Peter the apostle, said it like this: "Beloved, do not be surprised at the fiery trial when it comes upon you to test you, as though something strange were happening to you. But *rejoice* insofar as you share Christ's sufferings, that you may also rejoice and be glad when his glory is revealed" (1 Peter 4:12-13, author's emphasis). Peter is clearly telling us that difficult situations—he refers to these as "fiery trials"—are a normal part of life. However, in spite of the "suffering," Peter says to rejoice. We must realize that in spite of the fact that we will encounter unpleasant times in life we should still able to rejoice—to express the joy that God has given us. ❖

KEY 6B
Identify Joy Stealers

Even as we recognize that joy is a gift from God, we must simultaneously realize that there are things that would try to rob us of our joy. There are joy-thieves lurking all around us, waiting to make an effort to steal away our joy. Actually, there are plenty of such thieves. However, for the scope of this book, let's look at the two most prevalent: anxiety (worry) and discontentment.

Anxiety

"When anxiety was great within me, your consolation brought joy to my soul" (Psalm 94:19, NIV). It seems apparent from this verse that worry is directly opposed to joy.

Many years ago my wife, Barbara, and I read the classic book, *Pilgrim's Progress*, by John Bunyan, to our then-7-year-old son. (Okay, I'll admit it...we were reading the children's version, you know, the one *I* can understand.) In the story, Christian (Pilgrim in the original version) is journeying on the straight and narrow path to the celestial city. On his way he encounters many situations that parallel our lives as believers.

One of my most vivid recollections from the book occurred during a time when Christian was travelling with a fellow-sojourner named Hopeful. As they journeyed, they grew tired and decided to take a rest. Lying down in a meadow just off the path, Christian and Hopeful quickly fell asleep. While they were sleeping a giant named Despair awakened them and forced them to return with him to his castle. There he put them into his dungeon.

Once Christian and Hopeful were incarcerated, the giant showed them no mercy. He beat them. He refused to give them food or water. He showed them the bones of pilgrims who had died there before them. He even offered them poison to drink so that they could end their suffering. He tried to convince them that they may as well consume the toxic drink because they were going to die there like so many before them. At one point Christian was so distressed that he almost drank the poison, but Hopeful talked him out of it.

Finally, Christian remembered that earlier in the journey he had been given a key, known as the Key of

Promise. When he remembered the key, he quickly tried it in the lock of the dungeon door. With a bit of work he opened the door and Christian and Hopeful walked out, free.

Not long after reading this story I was given some very distressing news about our ministry's finances. Since, for all practical purposes, the ministry consists of Barbara and me, this news definitely affected me. It is not necessary to go into details, but suffice it to say that I was anxious. I was extremely worried about the final outcome.

The day after I received the news, I was in our home office working at a computer. Because of the worry about our finances my usual typing action was replaced by a rather pronounced banging on the keys of the computer keyboard. I made no attempt to hide the fact that I was upset. My wife, sensing my anxiety, said, "That giant, Despair, has really got a hold of you, hasn't he? Did you check your pocket for any keys?" With that particular illustration so recent and so vivid, her comment should have been enough to cause me to change my attitude. However, this particular day, I was not just anxious, I was engulfed in anxiety.

Because she did not receive the desired response from her comment, a while later she began to hum a favorite chorus. I knew the words very well and realized that the song was directed at me. The lyrics are:

> God is bigger than all my problems,
>   bigger than all my fears.

God is bigger than any mountain
that I can or cannot see.[1]

I finally realized she was right. She was inviting
me to choose joy. She knew I could still have joy even
in the midst of that very worrisome time. Guided by her
promptings, I jumped up from my desk and, in a very
positive way, said, "Okay, I'm getting it!" Right then
and there I chose joy. I made the decision not to allow
the joy-thief—anxiety—to steal away my joy. The situation was still the same, but my heart was changed. That
change of heart made all the difference. I chose to live
above the circumstances in life by choosing joy.

Immediately following Paul's injunction to the
Philippian church to, "Rejoice in the Lord always; again
I will say, Rejoice" he says this: "Do not be anxious
about anything, but in everything by prayer and supplication with thanksgiving let your requests be made
known to God" (Philippians 4:6). Paul tells us not to be
anxious and then goes on to explain how to avoid anxiety. He offers a simple two-step process:

1. "by prayer and supplication"—Pray and
commit the worrisome situation to God.
2. "with thanksgiving" — Thank Him
that He is in control of that predicament.

This sounds so simple. The truth is that we often
do both of these things. However, after we've done
them, we later snatch the situation back from the Lord

and attempt to deal with it (or at least worry about it) on our own. In doing so, we have just counteracted Paul's prescription for anxiety. So, what do we do instead?

When we recognize that we have taken the situation back from God, we must repeat the two-step process: we should once again commit the circumstance to the Lord and thank Him that he is in control of it. Even if it ultimately means repeating the same scenario 100 times in a day, eventually we will find victory over that joy-thief, anxiety.

Discontentment

The other major thief of our joy is discontentment. Truthfully, this one is probably even more of a problem for many people than worry. In part this is due to our society. Our culture thrives on making people feel not content in their present circumstances. There are even entire industries geared to increase our discontentment. Nearly every advertisement (television, radio, newspaper, magazine, etc.) has an underlying theme: the notion that if you do not possess their particular product, then your life is missing something. And where there is discontentment, joy is usually lacking.

We too often entertain thoughts like,

> "If I was just smarter (or faster, or prettier, or...)
> "If only I had done a better job with my kids..."
> "If I just had more money..."

"If only I would have worked harder in school..."
"If I weren't so disorganized..."
"If I only had a little more time..."
"If I would have gotten the present I *really* wanted for Christmas..."

All of these are discontentment. However, even possessing *all* of the things that seem to be lacking will not ultimately give real joy.

Actually, it appears as though having lots of possessions has the opposite effect. According to one recent survey, the U.S. is the unhappiest nation on earth. We have more mental disorders and depression per capita than anywhere else. Interestingly, according to the same survey, the happiest nation is Nigeria.

In the mid-nineties, teen idol and rocker Kurt Cobain committed suicide. At the height of his career—and at the ripe old age of 27—he shot himself in the head. He was extremely "successful." He had achieved money, power and fame. So why did he kill himself? His suicide note stated that he'd had it all and it hadn't satisfied him. He had not found contentment.

The truth is that you can possess all that this world has to offer, but it will never bring contentment. Only one thing will bring lasting contentment: a relationship with God through Jesus Christ. Nothing else will ultimately satisfy.

In the previous chapter we read about Paul writing to the Philippians that they should rejoice. Paul wrote that idea not just once in his letter but repeatedly. Here's the often-overlooked part of that story, though. Where was the Apostle Paul when he wrote those words? He was in prison. To me that changes the entire scenario. This is not some guy lounging pool-side at the Jerusalem Marriott, sipping ice-cold lemonade, and saying, "It's easy to rejoice, you guys. Look at me." No, this is incarcerated-for-following-Jesus Paul, saying, "If I can do it in here, surely you can do it out there. Rejoice!"

I hope you have heard of or read about Pastor Richard Wurmbrand. He has written several books, perhaps his most well-known being *Tortured for Christ*. He is also the founder of the powerful ministry, "Voice of the Martyrs." Wurmbrand was a Romanian pastor who suffered much persecution at the hands of the communists. He spent a great deal of time in prison because of his outspoken Christian faith. When he was imprisoned, he was often placed in solitary confinement to keep him from turning other prisoners to Christ. In his writing, he mentions that while in solitary confinement he was usually given just enough physical nourishment to keep him alive. Often it was a crust of bread and cup of dirty water for his day's rations. However, for real sustenance he would endeavor to call to mind as many passages of Scripture as he could and recite them aloud.

Once, as Wurmbrand sat alone in his cell in solitary confinement, he endeavored to recall Luke 6:22-23. He remembered the first part: "Blessed are you when people hate you and when they exclude you and revile you and spurn your name as evil, on account of the Son of Man!" He thought this section of Scripture was quite appropriate for his present situation. He felt excluded and reviled and spurned. Then he attempted to recollect the remainder of the passage. He was able to recall, "Rejoice in that day..." and "...for, behold your reward is great in heaven." Try as he might, though, Wurmbrand could not seem to bring to mind the section in between. He strained, trying to remember, wracking his brain for the missing words. He repeated the parts he could recall over and over, hoping to trigger the elusive words. Finally it worked. The missing words popped into his mind: "and leap for joy."

At this sudden recollection, Wurmbrand prayed, "Lord, Your word says it, so I'm going to do it." Emaciated and half-starved, he struggled to his feet and, with a little jump, declared, "I praise you Jesus." With that he got a little more vigor and jumped higher the next time. Soon, despite his physical condition and his confining circumstances he was leaping for joy, just as the Scripture had said. In fact, he was joyfully jumping all about in his small cell. He did not wallow in self-pity. Instead, he chose to release the joy that was already inside.

While Wurmbrand was leaping for joy a guard happened to look into the cell. The guard apparently thought Wurmbrand must have been on the verge of completely losing his mind because he immediately brought him an enormous platter of breads, meats and cheeses.

I would be in error to suggest that choosing joy in

difficult situations will always immediately and dramatically change the physical circumstances, as happened with Richard Wurmbrand. That could happen, but not necessarily. However, I can honestly tell you that when you choose joy, making that choice will change your heart, and, at least for you, that will change everything.

Most musicologists would agree that Ludwig van Beethoven was a premiere musician and composer. More than 150 years after his death, his music still inspires and entertains. His Ninth Symphony has been hailed by some as perhaps his finest work. It is all instrumental until near the end when one single baritone voice comes in chanting "Joy, joy..." (Actually it is in German so the word is *freude*, but it means "joy.") Soon others join in until an entire chorus of voices is singing, "Joy, joy..."

The first time the Ninth Symphony was ever performed it generated such enthusiasm that when the "Joy" section crescendoed, it was almost as though someone gave a command for the audience to rise to their feet and cheer. They applauded clamorously, but Beethoven did not even notice. Finally one of the singers leaned over and tapped Beethoven on the shoulder to show him. The reason he had not heard the commotion was simple: he was deaf. In fact, at that point he had been deaf for ten years.

I'm a mediocre musician, but I know lots of *really* talented musicians. I cannot even fathom what it must have been like for a musician the caliber of Beethoven to be deaf for ten years. He easily could have said that he was going to wait for more favorable circumstances in order to write about and exercise joy, but he didn't. Instead, even in the midst of what was seemingly the very worst that life had to offer, he still chose to express the joy that God had given. Beethoven had made the decision to live above life's circumstances by choosing to walk in joy.

Unfortunately, it is very easy in our culture to think that certain things are necessary for us to be content, to be fulfilled. The truth is, when we look for contentment in anything but God, we will always be disappointed. You may gain all that this world has to offer, but, apart from the Lord, it will never bring lasting contentment. Nothing except the relationship with our Creator, for which Jesus paid so dearly, will ultimately cause us to be fulfilled.

The idea of having joy in all circumstances is difficult for us because, quite honestly, it is contrary to years of training. In a very similar way, the Bible shows us that through decades of slavery under harsh taskmasters, the Israelites were trained to murmur and complain. Because of that, it was easy for them to lapse back into the complaining mode even after they had been rescued from slavery. We too, because of our thankless, joyless, discontented society, have become very adept at murmuring and complaining. Instead, we need to learn to choose joy in every situation.

Discontentment and anxiety will try to steal away your joy. Don't let them. Don't allow those joy-thieves to rob you. Instead, make the choice to express joy—it is, after all, a gift from God—regardless of the situation or circumstances.

If your joy seems to be waning, if you're finding it difficult to express joy, here are a few suggestions to get it back.

> 1. Meditate on the truth of God's Word. Throughout your day "chew" on Scriptures like 2 Corinthians 6:10, Psalm 118:24, Isaiah 61:10, Philippians 4:4 and others.
> 2. Ask God to fan into flame the joy of the Holy Spirit within you.
> 3. One of the best ways to renew joy is to play worship songs and sing along. (That brings us full circle, doesn't it?)
> 4. Finally, as I've said before, simply make the choice to rejoice. In spite of your circumstances decide to exercise the joy that the Lord has given you.

Making the decision to rejoice in the Lord means you are choosing to worship Him. Like the apostles after being flogged, like Pastor Richard Wurmbrand in solitary confinement, like Beethoven after ten years of deafness, choose to rejoice. Even in the midst of an unsettling scenario, we can still worship by expressing the joy that God has given us. ❖

KEY 7A

Keep Your Eyes on the Goal

Part of the reason that we often find it difficult to worship the Lord during difficult times is because we are so focused on the here and now. From our very narrow perspective, it can appear that what we can see is all there is. Our experience might suggest that this life that we live here and now is the entirety of everything. Carl Sagan, in his "documentary" *Cosmos*, offers an excellent—though sadly mistaken—summary of such an idea when he says, "The cosmos is all there is or ever was or ever will be."[1]

Peggy Noonan is a best-selling author of several books on politics, history and culture. She has a very different perspective on this issue.

> I think we have lost the old knowledge that
> happiness is overrated—that, in a way, life
> is overrated. We have lost, somehow, a
> sense of mystery—about us, our purpose,
> our meaning, our role. Our ancestors
> believed in two worlds, and understood
> *this* to be the solitary, poor, nasty, brutish
> and short one. We are the first generation
> of man that actually expected to find hap-
> piness here on earth, and our search for it
> has caused such unhappiness. The reason:
> If you do not believe in another, higher
> world, if you believe only in the flat mate-
> rial world around you, if you believe that
> this is your only chance at happiness—if
> that is what you believe, then you are not
> disappointed when the world does not give
> you a good measure of its riches, you are
> despairing.[2]

From a biblical perspective, Noonan's comment clearly is more accurate than Sagan's. Too many Christians think that their faith is only about the here and now. It's not. I have met believers who had the notion that if they weren't driving a brand new Mercedes, they didn't have enough faith. Because they drove only a fif-teen-year-old Ford, they were despairing.

The truth is that our Christian faith is not primarily about life here on earth. "If in this life only we have hoped in Christ, we are of all people most to be pitied" (1 Corinthians 15:19). When this life is over, we have something far greater waiting for us.

"But our citizenship is in heaven…" (Philippians 3:20). We are just aliens here. This world is not really our home. Our final—and eternal—destination is heaven.

In order to be able to worship God in the midst of adverse circumstances while we're still here on earth, we need to do what Scripture tells us to do. "Set your minds on things that are above, not on things that are on earth" (Colossians 3:2).

Okay, you might be thinking, *Sure, Tom, that's an easy thing to say, but a very difficult one to do.* It's true. It can be quite challenging to set your mind on something you've never seen, especially when there are real-life circumstances staring you in the face.

My wife, Barbara, is a meticulous housekeeper. Clutter and dirt do not generally last very long in our home. The weekly cleaning day restores pretty much the entire house to its pristine condition. Periodic spot cleanings throughout the week demonstrate her resolve to keep our home immaculate. It is a trait inherited from her full-blooded Dutch mother, and a trait that has been tested numerous times by her very messy husband.

Barb asked the Lord to show her how our knowledge of heaven should impact our lives. After all, the Bible says we should set our minds on things that are above, not on things that are on earth. So, my wife asked

God to teach her what the hope of heaven has to do with life here and now.

We were in the midst of a remodeling project, adding a new portion onto our home. The plastic sheeting between the present living space and the new addition was only minimally effective. Sawdust and drywall dust still found their way through somehow. The mud from around the new foundation seemed to take great delight in sneaking into the house on the shoes of our children. Once inside, of course, it loosed its hold on the shoes and dropped off onto the floors. Everywhere.

Obviously these newfound supplies of dust and grime were a major source of frustration for my wife. At times she gritted her teeth and smiled. Other times were worse. Then, one beautiful summer day the sun shone brightly through the windows and illuminated not only the fresh layer of dust on the furniture, but also the airborne particles that had yet to find their way to the furniture. My wife peered through the plastic sheeting at the place where our soon-to-be family room was located and thought, "Soon it will all be over and we'll be able to enjoy our home without all the mess." As these thoughts passed through her mind, she realized that this is how our hope of heaven should affect our lives now. Although there are trials and tribulations in this life—situations that make us uncomfortable and maybe even irritable—as we look forward to the promise of our new home—our real home in heaven—we can face those things with assurance that they are just fleeting inconveniences. Even in the midst of present day difficulties, we can still worship the Lord because of the hope of heaven.

During the late 1700s and into the 1800s, field slaves in the South were allowed, and even encouraged, to sing songs during their outdoor work. This was the case when they had to coordinate their efforts for hauling a fallen tree or moving a heavy load. But some "drivers" also allowed slaves to sing "quiet" songs, as long as the songs were not apparently against slaveholders. Such songs could be sung either independently or with an entire group.

What kind of life did those slaves really have? They had been kidnapped from their homeland and brought by ship to a strange new land, where they were forced to work, and work hard. At some point, though, many were introduced to the Savior. They knew freedom, albeit only on the inside. Their bodies were still enslaved. They were whipped and beaten. Heavy lifting and hard labor was their lot. If it was convenient—and financially lucrative—the masters could sell their relatives. Spouses or children were torn away and sent somewhere else. It must have been a horrendous situation.

Yet, in the midst of that scenario, they would sing. As I looked into this recently, I happened across a website that lists the lyrics of numerous songs sung by those slaves.[3] I was honestly surprised—although in retrospect I should not have been—by how many of those songs had heaven as the main theme.

The classic, of course, is "Swing Low, Sweet Chariot," but there were too many more to list them all.

A few highlights include:

"I Am Seeking for a City"
"Ain't Going to Tarry Here"
"Blow Your Trumpet, Gabriel"
"Oh What a Beautiful City"

I can imagine those slaves working in the fields singing back and forth with each other about heaven. "There is more than just this life, brother. Don't become beaten down in your soul by what happens here and now. Remember our real home is in heaven."

Those southern slaves sang of the hope that lay beyond this life. They kept their eyes on the goal. In the midst of their adverse circumstances, they looked toward the One who truly holds the future, and they worshiped Him in the midst of heartache and pain.

Let's look at this from a different angle for a moment. I love the fact that God interacts with His creation. Throughout my years here on Earth, I have personally seen the Lord's intervention in numerous situations. A life-threatening disease gone with no medical explanation. Financial crises completely and miraculously turned around. A relationship that had been totally and horrifically severed, repaired in a moment. Only the hand of the Almighty could have caused these upside-down situations to be righted again. Although human beings were involved in all of these, no human could have orchestrated such cataclysmic changes. It was clearly and obviously the work of the Most High.

Think for a moment, though, about the wonderful miracles that Jesus' original followers must have seen. Surely they were more amazing than the things that you and I have witnessed. When Jesus sent forth the seventy-two disciples, part of what they were told to do was "heal the sick" (Luke 10:9). When they returned, the disciples were beside themselves with excitement. "Lord, even the demons are subject to us in your name!" (Luke 10:17). Can you picture those enthusiastic missionaries jumping up and down and laughing as they shared their amazing experiences with Jesus?

Maybe one told about a man whose legs were bent at odd angles away from one another. Walking was not merely difficult, it was impossible. Then Beriah prayed and the man's legs snapped into the proper position. Everyone heard a loud crack and the man's legs looked like everyone else's. "It was absolutely amazing," whispered a still shocked Beriah.

Perhaps another told of a woman who was in such excruciating pain that she hadn't slept in two months. Her face, gaunt and ashen, appeared as though she had already died. But when Hanniel prayed, the woman fell to the ground in such a profound sleep that no one could awaken her for three days. When she finally did wake up, she was totally and completely healed. Tears streamed down the cheeks of Hanniel as he recounted the story to Jesus and the others.

Obviously these are simply my imaginings. However, I'm sure that my imaginings fall far short of the miracle-working power of God. After all, Scripture says that God is "able to do far more abundantly than all that we ask or think" (Ephesians 3:20). Those disciples surely saw and experienced the power of God and so they "returned with joy" (Luke 10:17).

In the midst of their excitement and enthusiasm, though, Jesus said this, "Nevertheless, do not rejoice in this, that the spirits are subject to you, *but rejoice that your names are written in heaven*" (Luke 10:20, author's emphasis).

As much as the miracles are spine-tingling events, the real excitement is reserved for the fact that we are headed for heaven. No matter how miraculous an earthly event may appear, it will never compare with our heavenly home with God.

In light of this, what will heaven be like? More amazing than blind eyes seeing. More astounding than deaf ears hearing. More wonderful than the lame walking or the dumb talking. More staggering than the physically dead being raised again to physical life. You and I, even in our most vivid, flamboyant and dramatically creative thoughts, still fall short of the reality of heaven. And, as we fix our eyes on those things that are yet to be revealed, we can still worship God even when the situations and circumstances of our lives here on earth are less than ideal.

Let's take some time in the next chapter to try to get a better picture of what heaven will be like. ❖

KEY 7B
Picturing Heaven

God created all that we know in six days. Jesus said that He was going to prepare a place for us (John 14:2-3). He's been working on it for 2,000 years. What will it be like? As Christians, that is our home. Not this puny, dull, lackluster planet called Earth, but the magnificence and splendor of the eternal home the Lord Himself has prepared for us.

A little girl was taking an evening walk with her father. Wonderingly, she looked up at the stars and exclaimed; "Oh, Daddy, if the wrong side of heaven is so beautiful, what must the right side be!" Until we're there, we can only imagine.

The Apostle John got to see heaven before he actually went there. He tried to describe his vision in the very last book of the Bible. Have you ever read the Revelation? I think John's words seem forced, as though he was limited by his vocabulary. "The city was pure gold, clear as glass" (Revelation 21:18). Gold that is clear? And what exactly is "a sea of glass"? (4:6). Or radiance like a rare jewel? (21:11) Or gates made from a single pearl? (21:21) Doesn't it seem as though John is reaching, trying to find something—anything—in our world and vocabulary to compare with what he has seen? But he can't. Not really. Oh, of course we can conjure up some ideas in our minds from John's words, but what did he really mean? What was it he actually saw? Are our imaginings even close to John's vision? I doubt it.

I have had the opportunity to see many wonders here on earth. I have beheld sunrises in Maine and sunsets in Hawaii. I've seen the vastness of an ocean from 35,000 feet in the air and peered through a microscope at a single-cell amoeba. I have stood at the edge of the Grand Canyon, awestruck by the grandeur. Mountains in Colorado and deserts in Arizona. Great rivers in the Midwest and glaciers in Alaska. Forests in Eastern Europe and wheat fields in Kansas. All of these and more are spectacular sights to behold. They brim with the obvious handiwork of the Creator, but all of them are only a foreshadowing. They are merely a taste of what awaits, a hint of that which lies ahead.

Father Glenn Sudano is part of the Community

of the Franciscan Friars of the Renewal in New York. Some time ago, Glenn wrote an interesting article entitled, "Almost Heaven." Although space does not permit inclusion of the entire article, here is a brief excerpt.

> While pouring my second cup of coffee, I ponder. The beautiful and pleasurable things in this world are gifts from God, therefore, they all are good. Yet when we only enjoy the gift, while ignoring the Giver, we get ourselves in trouble. The very things God created to be a blessing for us, then become a burden. What God made to catch our attention becomes a distraction. This is why, I suppose, God in His mercy designed us with a built-in breaker box; meaning, He created us with a limited capacity for earthly pleasure so as to not lose our desire for the delights of heaven.
>
> For example, two cups of coffee are fine, but how would I feel after downing two pots? A few slices of homemade pizza tastes heavenly; how would I feel after a few pies? —like hell! A twenty minute hot shower—*ahhh!* A twenty hour shower—*aggh!* I mean, how long could you enjoy a striking sunset, a brisk back massage, or blaring bag pipes? Yes, it's a question of capacity. On earth God

allows us to taste tiny crumbs which fall from the heavenly banquet table. He doesn't want us to spoil our appetite for the special supper He has prepared for His children.

Yes, what Dante did with pen and Michelangelo did with paint, we also must do, that is: imagine eternity. No doubt, if we seriously thought more of heaven, we might do better here on earth. The things we love in life are but bait the Master Fisherman uses to pull us up from our world to His. What do I love which makes me think and long for heaven? I love the smell of fresh Basil right off the bush or clean linen warm on the line. I love the sight of an elderly couple holding hands and an infant asleep in his mother's arms. I love the feel of a friend's warm embrace or a hot bath after a long winter's walk. I love the sound of children playing, or better yet, praying. Finally, I love the taste of almost anything homemade and eaten outside!

As Saint Paul wrote: "Eye has not seen nor has ear heard...*what God has prepared for those who love Him.*"[1]

Throughout my lifetime I had seen many pictures of fall foliage in New England. The photos were beautiful. Many people I've met have cherished wall hangings of such gorgeous scenery. The intensity of color can be striking and inspiring. The reds, oranges and yellows can almost seem surreal, as though someone imagined such vividness and tried to paint it. Such photos are beautiful to behold, but then I went to New England in autumn. Afterward, honestly, those photos seemed lifeless. Oh, they were nice, but once you've beheld the real thing, the photos are just…photos.

In the same way, the moments in my life that have brought such sweet fulfillment are just a dim reflection of the sweetness I will know in heaven. The most strikingly beautiful panorama I've seen here on earth is but a pale picture of the beauty of heaven.

The things that won't be in heaven

It is fascinating to consider the good things that we will experience in heaven. Perhaps just as important, though, are the things that we won't experience there. In the last two chapters of his revelation of Jesus Christ, the Apostle John tells us that numerous things we experience here and now will no longer exist in heaven. Most notably these include sorrow and crying, pain, the curse, night, and death. We will never experience any of those in heaven. So, on a practical level, what does this mean for you and me?

No sorrow or crying (Revelation 21:4)

Curt Coffield and Ed Kerr are popular worship

songwriters. One of the songs that they co-wrote, "The Healing Song," says this:

> They say that time heals all wounds,
> but I beg to differ.
> For there are these hurts in my heart
> I haven't got over.
> Thought I'd forgotten,
> thought I forgave,
> but when I look deep inside me
> I can still sense the pain.[2]

I think Curt and Ed are right. Time really doesn't heal all wounds. My father passed away more than a quarter century ago. Guess what? There are times even now that I miss him, times I wish he was still here. But he's not.

More than a decade ago I was wronged in a big way. Someone did something that completely and inalterably changed the course of my life. At the time I was devastated. Many times over the years, though, I have made the decision to forgive. But guess what? In the quiet moments, if I look into the inner recesses of my heart, there is still something there. Oh, I'm not devastated any longer. I have clearly seen the hand of God turn the situation for His glory. Today I am able to echo the words that Joseph spoke to his brothers in the Old Testament, "As for you, you meant evil against me, but God meant it for good" (Genesis 50:20). At the same time, though, the darkness of my own heart—the holding on to that which is not mine to hold—is still too evident. There is sorrow in this life, and sometimes crying.

In heaven, though, it's all gone. No more heartache. No more if-only's. No more yearning for the way things used to be. No longing for those who are gone. No spilled milk. No regrets. No sorrow at all. Not even a little. Even more amazingly, God Himself will wipe away every tear (Revelation 21:4).

If you've ever cried in the middle of the night from a seemingly-inconsolable sorrow—the hurt of loss and heart-ache—that caused tears to well up from deep within, then you are a prime candidate for the ministrations and compassion of a tear-wiping God. Perhaps your mother or someone else very close to you has held you and encouraged you to cry and "let it all out." Even then, though, you've never known the depth of compassion that God Himself will show you in heaven.

No pain (Revelation 21:4)

I don't know about you, but I thank God for doctors. Medical physicians, doctors of dentistry, and chiropractors have all helped me and various members of my family through some physically trying times. Their knowledge of the human body and how to fix what's wrong has been a big comfort on many occasions.

My sister had major headaches for years. Some days she was unable to function at all. After years of searching, she finally found a clinic that offered her not only hope, but real help. It took a while, and she's not totally cured yet, but she is light-years better than she was before. She still has some pain, but it is minimal compared to what she previously experienced.

My mom has arthritis in her hands and wrists. Not just a little touch of it occasionally but full-blown, all-the-time arthritis. The kind where the painful cortisone shots directly into the wrist were worth it because it made the real pain diminish. Eventually, though, the shots were no longer helpful. She was in such pain that she finally had to have a wrist-replacement on one arm, and the other wrist surgically fused in place. Mom is also a quilter. Quilting steps that she once could do in a matter of moments now take much longer, and that's not to mention the pain involved in doing those steps.

I won't bore you with my root-canal-gone-bad story, but I've never experienced such pain before or since. This from the guy who had stitches in his head at least six different times before reaching the age of ten. I've known my share of pain.

Pain is a part of this life. Many of us, especially as we get older, have simply learned to live with it. After all, what else can you do? But in heaven, it's all gone. No more pain. No more little nagging muscle aches. No more broken fingers. No more paper cuts. No more slivers. No more ingrown toe-nails. No more cancer. No more migraines. No pain at all. It's gone. It's all gone. That's heaven. For eternity.

No curse (Revelation 22:3)

When God booted Adam and Eve out of the Garden, He said, "...cursed is the ground because of you; in pain you shall eat of it all the days of your life; thorns and thistles it shall bring forth for you...By the sweat of your face you shall eat bread, till you return to the ground, for out of it you were taken; for you are dust, and to dust you shall return" (Genesis 3:17-19).

This was the curse: life was going to be difficult. Up until then, Adam and Eve had it easy. Life was a bowl of cherries. And you can bank on the fact that those pre-curse cherries were far more delicious than any you or I have ever tasted. Not only that, but they didn't need to go searching for them through tangled vines and thorns. I picture trees bursting with the largest, most flavorful fruits and nuts ever dreamed up by the creative mind of the Creator. Not only that, but God Himself was there to keep them company. They had it made.

Unfortunately, it all changed in an instant. God cursed the ground and everything was altered from the roots up. Now it would be work—and lots of it—finding and harvesting whatever they needed to eat. They would have to till the ground, plant and fertilize, and still the plants would be far less nutritious, far less colorful, far less flavorful than anything they had before the fall. It must have been heartbreaking and demoralizing. They knew what they had before and what they had afterward. There was no comparison.

Further, from the moment of the curse, Adam's and Eve's own bodies began to decay along with everything else. Did they notice a difference when they got out of bed in the morning? Maybe their arms and legs didn't work quite as well as they did previously. Perhaps their eyesight became somewhat blurred or dimmed. Of course, I'm only speculating here, but it certainly seems likely in light of God's words. Seemingly everything had been turned on its head. Nothing was quite like it used to be.

Here's the good news, though. In heaven everything is restored. The curse is gone. No more heavy lifting. No more shortness of breath. No more thorns or thistles or rotten apples. No more sweat.

I enjoy cooking, but I really like to go out to eat or go to someone's house for a meal. In those cases, I generally don't need to work to make the meal happen. I can relax and let someone else take care of it. In various places in Scripture, heaven is referred to as a sumptuous feast (Matthew 8:11; Luke 14:15; Revelation 19:9, 17). Of course we can not say with certainty that this is a literal meal with food or if these are simply allegorical statements. Either way, there is no indication in any of them that we will need to work for the feast. We are merely invited guests. No need to go to the garden to pick some beans. (Or even to till the garden in order to plant the beans!) No need to clean up the grill in order to prepare for cooking. No work. No sweat. It's all done.

That's heaven. The curse is eradicated, completely and totally removed. The good stuff is restored and the bad stuff is gone. All of it. Forever.

No night (Revelation 22:5)

Most people find night frightening, at least at

times. Things that go bump in the night scare us. During the daylight hours, when we can see everything much more clearly, we are less apt to be afraid. The shadows and darkness of the night can be disconcerting. For many, night time can be a very scary time.

Interestingly, night is often symbolic of evil in the Bible. The phrase "songs in the night" (Job 35:10; Psalm 77:6) uses night to signify trials and trouble. In 1 Thessalonians 5:5, we are referred to as children of the day and this is contrasted with not belonging to night or darkness. ("For you are all children of light, children of the day. We are not of the night or of the darkness.") Further, when the adversaries came to seize Jesus in the Garden, He said, "When I was with you day after day in the temple, you did not lay hands on me. But this is your hour, and the power of darkness" (Luke 22:53). Another translation says, "But this is your hour—when darkness reigns." Both from a biblical perspective as well as an experiential perspective, night and darkness often represent an evil that we would prefer to avoid.

As Christians, though, we have something better to which we look forward. The old hymn, "On Jordan's Stormy Banks I Stand," speaks of heaven like this:

> All o'er those wide extended plains
> shines one eternal day;
> there God, the Son, forever reigns,
> and scatters night away.[3]

Puritan Ezekiel Hopkins lived during the seventeenth century. He described heaven in this manner: "Where the unveiled glories of the Deity shall beat full upon us, and we forever sun ourselves in the smiles of God."

In heaven there is no night. All of the dark things of this life—sin, wickedness, corruption, trials and troubles—will be gone. No night. No darkness. No evil. No hardships. No distresses. Just the glorious light—goodness and unending love—of God. There is indeed a light at the end of the tunnel, an unending light of the mercy of the Lord.

No death (Revelation 21:4)

Not long ago I had a heart scan. I was experiencing no symptoms of any sort of heart problems, but my dad had his first heart attack when he was younger than I am now. I just wanted to check, to make sure that I am okay. Somehow, the older I get, the more inevitable death seems. It's going to happen to me someday. I'm going to die. And, I don't want to alarm you, but so are you.

Over the years I have met many people who have lost children. Maybe it was an accident. Perhaps an illness. Whatever the cause, most times the parents still bear a great deal of pain. Of course they do. What parent wouldn't? I can not even imagine what it would be like for one of my children to die. How much more devastating could life get than that? Death causes a separation, one for which we generally are unprepared.

Some of my greatest heroes—those who have meant so much in shaping my life and my walk with

God—have died. Their passing was not easy. I cried when I heard the news. My father died just six months after I got married. Death is a very real and inevitable part of our existence here on earth.

Perhaps you, too, have been ravaged by the death of someone close. If so, I've got some really good news, and it has nothing to do with saving money on car insurance. In heaven, death is gone. It is banished, and not just for a short time. We will not simply experience a brief respite from death, only to have it return with a vengeance. No, death will be no more. Ever. No one will ever die in heaven. Death, and even the effects of death, will be permanently, unendingly gone.

> He will swallow up death forever; and the Lord GOD will wipe away tears from all faces, and the reproach of his people he will take away from all the earth, for the LORD has spoken. It will be said on that day, "Behold, this is our God; we have waited for him, that he might save us. This is the LORD; we have waited for him; let us be glad and rejoice in his salvation." (Isaiah 25:8-9)

God Himself will dwell with them

I love the story of Solomon's Temple. God had told David that his son would build a temple. Consequently, Solomon gladly took on the task. The events leading up to the construction—including obtaining the necessary materials—were obviously orchestrated and blessed by God. The construction itself was carried out with such precision and on such a grand scale that, even today with thousands of years of advancement in construction practices and techniques, such an undertaking would still be monstrous. How much more so was it back then? How they accomplished such an amazing feat with no modern equipment is beyond me. Surely the Lord was with His people through each step of the process.

From the descriptions in Scripture, the opulence and attention to detail in the completed project must have been breathtaking. What must it have been like to see walls overlaid with pure gold? The altar, the Ark of the Covenant, the laver—all of the various pieces of furniture were carefully designed and meticulously constructed.

Then, at the dedication of the temple came the real coup de grâce: God's presence filled the temple in such a powerful way that the priests could not even remain standing to fulfill their duties. The Lord Almighty, Who made heaven and earth, indwelt the temple in a real and tangible way. God had obviously blessed this project from start to finish. Because He repeatedly gave His stamp of approval, it is clear that this temple was something that the Lord wanted in place.

However, let me toss you another perspective. God really did *not* want this temple to be built. Actually, He didn't even want the *need* for the temple. In the Garden of Eden, Adam and Eve needed no temple. There was nothing between them and God. No barriers.

No need for priests or intermediaries. They had direct access to the Lord. It was only when sin entered the picture that there came a need for a temple. Though the Lord revealed Himself in a powerful way at the temple, it was second best. A stop-gap measure. Plan B. Though it is true that God worked powerfully in and through the temple, I think He mourned the necessity of it. His original plan, unobstructed fellowship between God and man, was really His first choice.

What must the relationship have been like between the Lord and Adam and Eve before sin? Unhindered. No need for a go-between. No necessity for smoke or incense or burnt offerings or sacrifices of any kind. A real face-to-face relationship. What was that like?! We can only imagine. Honestly, I am certain that our most vivid imaginings still fall far short of the reality.

Guess what, though. That's what heaven will be like! There will be nothing between us and our Creator. No sin. No fear. No regrets. All those things will be gone and we will behold the wonders of the King. All His glory and splendor will be revealed. No more seeing through a glass darkly. We will look upon Him with unveiled faces.

Noted Christian author and apologist, Os Guiness said it like this: "After all the years of hearing only the voice, we are about to see the face and feel the arms."[4] God Himself will dwell with us.

The end is really the beginning

C.S. Lewis said, "Has this world been so kind to

you that you should leave with regret? There are better things ahead than any we leave behind." Do you like the foretaste, the preliminary, the appetizer? If so, then you're going to love the main course.

George Whitefield was the foremost human leader of the Great Awakening, and a compatriot, friend and fellow-minister with John and Charles Wesley. Whitefield said, "How sweet is rest after fatigue! How sweet will heaven be when our journey is ended." When this life is done, the rest we have waiting for us cannot even begin to be described in human terms.

My wife and I had the privilege of singing at my father's funeral. After lots of deliberation, we finally chose a song made popular by B.J. Thomas, "Home Where I Belong." In part, it says this:

> When I'm feeling lonely,
> when I'm feeling blue,
> it's such a joy to know that I am
> only passing through.
> I'm headed home,
> I'm going home where I belong.[5]

Home. Where there will be no more sorrow or pain or death or evil or darkness or troubles or hardships or disease or trials or sin or curse or tears…ever again. And God Himself will dwell with us. You and I…we're going home.

As compelling as the descriptions of heaven that I've just offered may be, they only scratch the surface.

The real thing will be beyond human words... and human imagination. Best of all, it's real. Because of what Jesus has done—reconciling us to the Father—we can confidently look forward to our home in heaven. Doesn't that make you want to worship Him here and now? Doesn't that put whatever trials and difficulties we might face in this life into proper perspective? Take a moment right now—won't you?—and worship the Lord for giving us the promise of heaven with Him for eternity. ❖

Conclusion
Worshiping God in the Hard Times

It seems to me that people in the past and even people from impoverished nations today understand suffering and difficulties better than we do. Face it: We're spoiled. Our nation has lived in relative ease throughout most of our lifetimes. Ongoing hard times are foreign to the vast majority of us.

Charles Spurgeon, prolific preacher and author from the 1800s, wrote extensively about Christians and difficult times. In his *Morning & Evening Devotional*, Spurgeon said this:

Give a man wealth; let his ships

bring home continually rich freights; let the winds and waves appear to be his servants to bear his vessels across the bosom of the mighty deep; let his lands yield abundantly: let the weather be propitious to his crops; let uninterrupted success attend him; let him stand among men as a successful merchant; let him enjoy continued health; allow him with braced nerve and brilliant eye to march through the world, and live happily; give him the buoyant spirit; let him have the song perpetually on his lips; let his eye be ever sparkling with joy—and the natural consequence of such an easy state to any man, let him be the best Christian who ever breathed, will be *presumption...* Brother, beware of the smooth places of the way; if you are treading them, or if the way be rough, thank God for it. If God should always rock us in the cradle of prosperity; if we were always dandled on the knees of fortune; if we had not some stain on the alabaster pillar; if there were not a few clouds in the sky... we should become intoxicated with pleasure, we should dream "we stand;" and stand we should, but it would be upon a pinnacle; like the man asleep upon the mast, each moment we should be in jeopardy.

We bless God, then, for our afflictions; we thank Him for our changes; we
extol His name for losses of property; for
we feel that had He not chastened us thus,
we might have become too secure.[1]

Spurgeon is right, of course. When everything is
going our way we can indeed become too secure in our
own position, rather than finding our security in Him.

We all love the story of the first thanksgiving. We
enjoy the fact that the Native American, Squanto, helped
the Pilgrims learn to plant and fish and hunt in this new
land. Their bountiful harvest was indeed a reason to celebrate. Honestly, though, how many of us think about that
grand day of giving thanks in its full context?

Captain Myles Standish was hired by the
Pilgrims as military advisor for their Plymouth Colony
in America. He eventually became a full member as
well as a valued leader of the community. Standish had
come to the "New World" with his wife, Rose, with high
expectations. When Rose became ill, however, he did
his best to spend as much time as possible at her bed-
side. That wasn't easy, though. That first winter in
Plymouth was harsh. With endeavoring to find food,
guarding against natives and cutting trees to build
homes, he had little time to spare.

William Bradford described the scene in his
History of Plymouth Plantation:

Then the sicknes begane to fall sore

> amongst them, and the weather so bad ....
> the Gov'r and cheefe of them, seeing so
> many dye, and fall downe sick dayly,
> thought it no wisdom to send away the
> ship....[2]

The winds were bitter and blew through every crack in the Mayflower as she lay anchored in the harbor. Rose's chills turned to uncontrollable shaking and then turned to blazing fever. The crude medicines they had available did little to ease her discomfort. By spring, Rose had died, along with so many others. Thirteen of the original eighteen wives who had set sail were no longer among the living.

What must that have been like? Try to imagine such a scenario. Of the 110 Pilgrims and ship's crew who left for America, more than half died that first winter. The pain of children and spouses dying—not just one or two but so many—from sickness and lack of food...such pain would not be simple to overcome. It could easily last for years. If they allowed it to, such pain could have completely consumed them.

The high hopes that Myles and Rose Standish had brought to the new world were gone, evaporated into grief. Yet that next autumn, Captain Standish joined the other Pilgrims—who undoubtedly still mourned those who had passed on—to give thanks for a bountiful harvest. In the midst of their pain, they celebrated and gave thanks to God.

The famous Bible commentator, Matthew

Henry, was once accosted by thieves and robbed. Following the incident, he wrote in his diary:

> Let me be thankful, first, because I was never robbed before; second, because although they took my money, they did not take my life; third, because although they took my all, it was not all that much; and, fourth, because it was I who was robbed, not I who robbed.

As a Bible Commentator, Matthew Henry surely knew that 1 Thessalonians 5:18 says to "give thanks in all circumstances." He was, in this instance, not only commenting on the Scriptures, but living them out in everyday life.

Whenever you or I face hard times in life, we also face a choice. Will we allow those difficulties to push us away from the Lord? Or, instead, will we choose to press in closer, worshiping Him anyway? The choice is ultimately ours. No one else can make the decision for us.

I pray that as you have read these pages you've been inspired to worship God no matter the situation. When life turns tragic, draw near to the One who created and redeemed you, the One who will ultimately take you home to be with Himself. Worship Him in the midst of adversity and you will find strength and confidence and joy you could never know otherwise. ❖

Notes

Chapter 3

1. Some have balked at my suggestion of blood, since the text does not mention blood. It's true the text does not specifically mention blood. But several verses later the jailer "washed their wounds." If there were no open wounds (i.e., bleeding), then what was the point of washing the wounds?

Chapter 4

1. It was actually Judah, the southern kingdom, but the people were, for the sake of simplicity in this writing, Israelites.

2. If they were mourning because they realized that they were in opposition to God, then their mourning was completely appropriate. However, my reading of the text gives me the impression that their mourning was in self-pity. They had been uprooted from their homeland and forced into slavery...

and they lamented that fact.

3. Charles R. Swindoll, *David*, W Publishing Group, Nashville, TN, 1997, pg. 34

Chapter 8

1. Mark Altrogge, "As Long as You Are Glorified," ©2008 Sovereign Grace Praise (BMI). Sovereign Grace Music, a division of Sovereign Grace Ministries. From *Come Weary Saints*. All rights reserved. International copyright secured. North American administration by Integrity Music. International administration by CopyCare International. Used by permission.

Chapter 9

1. Wayne Jacobsen, *He Loves Me!*, Windblown Media, Newbury Park, CA, 2007, pg. 92

Chapter 10

1. Charles Spurgeon, *Spurgeon's Morning & Evening Devotional*, December 16 AM

2. Lisa Qualsett and Sue Christensen, "All That Remains," ©2008 Highland Park Evangelical Free Church, Columbus, Nebraska. Used by permission.

Chapter 11

1. http://www.nlag.net/Sermons/Transcripts/mjthanks.htm

Chapter 12

1. public domain, from "Close to Thee" written in 1874 by Fanny Crosby

2. http://www.wholesomewords.org/biography/bcrosby3.html

3. public domain, from "To God Be the Glory" written in 1875 by Fanny Crosby

Chapter 14

1. Tim Hansel, *You Gotta Keep Dancin'*, pg 55

Chapter 15

1. Gordon Jensen, "Bigger Than Any Mountain," ©1976 Jensen Music

Chapter 16

1. Sagan, Carl (Producer). (1980). *Cosmos*. Los Angeles, CA: Cosmos Studios.

2. Peggy Noonan, quoted by Joseph M. Stowell in *Eternity*, Chicago, Illinois: Moody Press, 1995.

3. http://www.negrospirituals.com/news-song/index.htm

Chapter 17

1. Fr. Glenn Sudano, excerpted from an article entitled, "Almost Heaven," on http://www.franciscanfriars.com

2. Curt Coffield and Ed Kerr, "The Healing Song," ©2000 & 2003 Like-a-Card Praise and Kerrtunes

3. public domain, "On Jordan's Stormy Banks I Stand" by Samuel Stennett

4. Os Guinness, *The Call*, (Nashville, Tennessee: Word Publishing, 1998), pg. 244.

5. Pat Terry, "Home Where I Belong," ©1976 Pat Terry

Conclusion

1. Charles Spurgeon, *Morning & Evening Devotional*, March 10 AM

2. William Bradford, *William Bradford's History of Plymouth Plantation, 1606-1646*, pg. 115